Manhood

Letters from readers of the first edition

From men:

- [Manhood] *has given me the first inkling in my life of what it is to be an integrated, self-respecting man.*
- *My mate sent a copy to his two brothers who never contact him. One rang the next day and wanted to talk and thank him for sending the book.*
- *It finally gave me the courage to approach my father and mother, and sort things out ... I feel lighter, happier, freer, healthier, emotionally and physically.*
- *At last someone has been able to state clearly what is happening inside our hearts.*
- *I can honestly say your book was the most important I've ever read.*
- *It's 6 am. I couldn't sleep, and got up at 3.30 and finished* Manhood. *What a blast !*
- Manhood *is a wonderful book. It made me cry. It crystallised and explained so many things.*
- *I finished reading your book, and went to where my little daughter and wife were playing in the living room. I got down and cried on my wife's chest, the first time I have cried for many years.*

From women:

- *What brought tears to my eyes was the fact that a man had written it. I hope the Men's Movement will turn the tide for all of us.*
- *It would be true to say that* Manhood *has transformed how I see my husband and father. It moved me to tears many times. It has brought us closer than ever.*
- *I felt it uncovered the deep longings all of us have for some kind of balance, purpose, meaning to our living and loving.*
- *I have watched my husband struggling for so many years, Now I feel there is a way forward for him, and he has begun his rejuvenation.*
- *I treasure your words and insight. I feel more compassion towards my husband and clearer about my son's needs.*
- *I don't know if this letter can possibly convey how I feel.*
- *As a committed feminist, I welcome this book.*

Manhood

Second edition

An action plan for changing
men's lives

Steve Biddulph

FINCH PUBLISHING
SYDNEY

MANHOOD: (Second edition) An action plan for changing men's lives
First edition published in 1994. This second edition published in 1995 by Finch Publishing Pty Limited, ACN 057 285 248, P O Box 120, Lane Cove, NSW 2066, Australia.

97 10 9 8 7

National Library of Australia
Cataloguing-in-publication entry

Biddulph, Steve.
  Manhood: an action plan for changing men's lives.

  2nd ed.
  Bibliography.
  ISBN 0 646 26144 4.

  1. Men's movement. 2. Men – Psychology. 3. Men – Mental health. I. Title.

305.32

Photographs by David Hancock.
Cover and text design by Steve Miller/Snapper Graphics.
Typeset by DOCUPRO, Sydney.
Printed by McPherson's Printing Group, Melbourne.

Contents

Acknowledgements

The many men who raised me.

George Biddulph, my father, who was a safe man to be around, and brought us to a warmer place.

Arthur John, Brian Caldwell and all teachers everywhere who know the value of praise and of going beyond the syllabus.

Tim Haas, John Morris and Graham Perkin – early mentors who believed in me when I wasn't so sure.

Robin Maslen, who told me about the Men's Movement and is a father figure to many people.

Colin Mackenzie, for giving me a professional start.

Ken and Elizabeth Mellor, for a seven-year apprenticeship in being clear.

Thakur Balak Bramachiri, in Calcutta, an exemplary elder, who embodied the concept of fathering as community action.

My friends, especially Lee Hodge, Geoff Best and the Supervision and Practitioner groups at the Collinsvale Centre.

The Tas CISD team. Mike Geeves. Mike Sharpe. The Taylor family. Neil Shillito and Simon McCulloch.

Rex Finch, publisher of Finch Publishing. Rex has steered four of our books into the hands of readers around the world. He is an exceptionally patient, energetic man, with an eye for detail that is frightening! It delights me that he has made the Men's Movement part of his own heart-work.

Laurie Goldsworthy for the eagle image and what it represents.

Everyone in the Green Movement worldwide.

Dave Hancock for his earthy and beautiful photographs on the cover and throughout the book, and for his encouragement.

Dr Rex Stoessiger of the Tasmanian Education Consortium for including me in his teacher seminars which helped to develop the section on boys in school.

Cec Craft and Elizabeth Shannon, both at the University of Tasmania – good friends who guided me on women's perspectives and gave encouragement.

Dawson Ruhl introduced me to the Duluth Model.

Paul Whyte helped me understand several aspects of raising boys.

Bettina Arndt has helped the book immeasurably by speaking and writing about it to her thousands of listeners and readers. She has a generous and courageous heart.

All the people who organise our seminars, especially Judi Taylor and her family.

The Men's Movement has brought me so many friends at such a

deep level. Wes Carter of Menswork and John Allan, David Mowaljarlai and Rein van de Ruit of The Circle of Men, Stuart and Ken at Life and Depth, and many other exemplary men give me hope for the world changing.
Finally, the part played in my work and in my life by my partner Shaaron Biddulph is inestimable. Shaaron is part of everything I do that is kind and strong.
And to our children, who teach us more everyday and are good enough reason to change the world.

Permissions

Grateful acknowledgement is made to the following people and organisations for permission to include their material in this book.
All quoted matter by Robert Bly in this book, unless otherwise stated, is taken from his book, *Iron John*. This material is reproduced with the kind permission of the publishers, Element Books of Shaftesbury, Dorset, UK.
'Male Bashing' which first appeared in *To Be A Man*, K.Thompson (editor) is reproduced with the kind permission of the author, Fredric Hayward, MR Inc., PO Box 163180, Sacramento, California, USA 95816.
The interview with Charles Perkins is extracted from 'The Return to The Dreamtime', with the permission of the author, Mr Stuart Rintoul, and the *Australian* newspaper.
The Wheels of Power-and-Control and Equality are reproduced with the permission of the Minnesota Program Development Incorporated Domestic Abuse Intervention Project, 206 West Fourth Street, Minnesota, 55806, USA.
The cartoon, 'Trouble at the I'm OK, You're OK Corral', is reprinted with kind permission of The Cartoonist Limited, London.
The cartoon, 'The Demon', is reprinted from *A Bunch of Poesy*, by Michael Leunig, with the kind permission of Collins/Angus & Robertson Publishers, a division of HarperCollins Publishers Australia.
Sources for brief quotations are given in the bibliography. Where other quotations have been used, every reasonable effort has been made to seek permission and include full accreditation of the source prior to publication.
The eagle image on the back cover is courtesy of Laurie Goldsworthy. This is a juvenile Tasmanian wedgetailed eagle, photographed in flight over the Great Western Tiers, Tasmania. Only about seventy-five successful breeding pairs of this Tasmanian subspecies (*Aquila audax fleayi*) remained in 1994. Loss of nesting habitat is the greatest threat to their survival.

Preface

Over forty thousand people bought the first edition of *Manhood*, and the warmth of men's and women's responses to the book has been literally overwhelming. I feel like I have launched in a hang-glider – exhilarated and scared at the same time. It's up – I hope I can fly it!

When the book was released in 1994 a stream of remarkable letters began, from men and women of all ages, saying 'thanks', 'this book tells my story', 'this is my life'. These were intense, detailed letters, often with reams of pages. I am still working to reply to them all. None of my earlier books have had such an emotional response. Booksellers everywhere told us of people coming back for more copies, to give their friends. Copies were sent – laden with meaning – to family members. Men wrote to me – 'My brother sent me this book. We've begun to talk about it'. 'I sent this book to my dad. Here is what he wrote back to me.' A high school principal in Perth gave copies to each of his forty staff. A social worker in Brisbane bought three hundred copies.

People made changes, too. They quit jobs, sold over-mortgaged houses, found out the truth about their childhoods, and made new and better bonds with their children and partners. Men began to feel good again about being men, and women told me they had begun to understand men better. One woman said that if she had read this book first, she would not have got divorced. Now she understood why her husband felt the way he did. In the larger world, changes are happening in how we see and treat men. Instead of droning on endlessly about 'the battle of the sexes', the media is beginning to understand and clarify the situation of boys, young men and adult men, and the focus is on positive, caring action.

I don't think *Manhood* alone is responsible for any of this, but it has had a leadership role, in 'giving people a better map of the road we are on'. Confusion and loneliness are always the great enemies in life, and the book has helped many men see their lives more clearly and discover that they were normal after all. It speaks to the common experience of men. One man told me, 'The bit about leaving one testicle behind in the bank manager's office, that was the part that got to me!'

Early on I had intended to write a book explaining the wonderful but obscure writings of Robert Bly – the poet who 'started' (as much as anyone) today's Men's Movement. *Manhood* was to be a kind of 'Bly-for-Beginners'. People now tell me they want 'less Bly, more Biddulph'. But the roots of the book lie in this deep compost, and I want to honour that, while also going into new terrain. *Manhood* is a distinctively Australian book, and part of the ongoing development of the Australian man.

May it give you hope and joy on your part of the journey.

Steve Biddulph
Spring, 1995

1
The Problem

Most men don't have a life. Instead, we have just learned to pretend. Much of what men do is an outer show, kept up for protection.

Most women today are not like this. They act from inner feeling and spirit, and more and more they know *who they are* and *what they want*. Little children of both sexes start out well – they are alive to themselves, expecting to be joyful, expecting life to be an adventure. But a boy's spirit begins to shrivel very early in life, until (often as not) he loses touch with it completely. By the time he becomes a man, he is like a tiger raised in a zoo – confused and numb, with huge energies untapped. He feels that there must be more, *but does not know what that more is*. So he spends his life pretending to be happy – to himself, his friends and his family.

Sometimes there is a breakthrough in this pretence. Sometimes we men get a taste of what life could be like or experience moments of real passion and glory in being alive. It can happen in surprising ways – surviving a traffic accident unscathed, finding yourself alone on a stretch of beach, having a certain kind of moment with a woman, being reunited with your children after time apart. We glimpse something, unsettling but beautiful ... and then the moment passes. We don't know how to bring it back. The sheer intensity just serves to frighten us, upsets the charade we have constructed as a stage set for our lives. Not sure what to do, we quickly go back to pretending everything is okay. We pretend and we wait and hope things will improve.

Not all men can stand to wait or to keep up the pretence:

- A school teacher in Hobart, rejected by his wife, walks into the sea late at night. He wears a diver's weight belt, the quick-release weights wired up so that he will have no chance to scrabble free. In seconds he is submerged in the dark water. His body, blue and swollen, washes in on the morning tide.
- A seventeen-year-old boy in Melbourne, top of his school, gains distinctions in only five of his six HSC subjects. (He has studied so hard that he makes small errors in the exams, through sheer fatigue.) He buys a shotgun, sneaks it home and that night, on the riverbank by his home, puts the barrel into his mouth and tilts back his head.
- A young man watches a celebrity 'lingerie parade' in a department store in Adelaide. There is high-energy music playing and orchestrated hysteria. As he watches, he cannot resolve the conflicting feelings of shame and arousal that swirl through his body. What does it mean – these erotic posturings from women who will give him no love? Agitated, he climbs onto the stage, shouts abuse and is dragged away by security guards. Half an hour later he jumps to his death from a nearby building.

Men are hurting. They are also hurting others. Physical violence against spouses, and a horrific incidence of child sexual abuse, point to something badly wrong with large numbers of men. Then there is the stuff of front page news – sexual abductions and murders of women and children, shopping mall massacres and the like.

Men, always men. As Robert Bly says, 'Are you depressed enough already?'

What is wrong with men?

There are questions we must ask about these situations. Are they just the rough edges where the fabric of a basically healthy society has accidentally unravelled? Or is there a flaw in the whole weave and all men so loosely connected that they hover on the edge of destruction or oblivion? Put another way: Have we no idea how to turn boys into safe, healthy, life-loving men?

Recently a Men's Movement has arisen that offers a clearer analysis of what has gone wrong for men and how to fix it. Instead of plugging on in quiet desperation – just toughing it out – there is a feeling in the air that men can learn to be happier, better people and that (incredible as it may sound) it can be a positive thing to be a guy! We men are not the monsters of the earth after all – at least not by choice. Men's Movement writers have pointed out what now seems obvious, although we never noticed it before – that boys in our society are horrendously **under-fathered** and are not given the processes or the mentor figures to help their growth into mature men. With no deep training in masculinity, boys' bodies get bigger, but they don't have the inner changes to match. They grow into **phony men** who act out a role – a complete facade which does not really work in any of life's arenas. (Girls, for all the obstacles put in their way, at least grow up with a continuous exposure to women at home, at school and in friendship networks. From this they learn a communicative style of womanhood that enables them to get close to other women and give and receive support throughout their lives.) Men's and boys' friendship networks are awkward and oblique, lacking in intimacy and often short term.

Boys and young men never know the inner world of older men, so each boy makes up an **image** based on the externals, TV, and peers which he then acts out to 'prove' he is a man.

Just as a chameleon bases its colour on its surroundings and has no 'true' colour, so men often have very little sense of their true selves. Whether they are faking the 'Sensitive New Age Guy' or clinging to the John Wayne, Fifties, tough-guy image, boys and men are equally lost and unhappy. The lack of help to grow into a man and the resulting desperate clinging to an 'I'm fine' facade has disastrous consequences. Not putting too fine a point on it, *men are a mess*. The terrible effects on our marriages, fathering abilities, our health and our leadership skills are a matter of public record. *Our marriages fail, our kids hate us, we die from stress and on the way we destroy the world!*

The three enemies

The Men's Movement begins with acknowledging the pain and grief that men feel, because this has been skimmed over for so long by men themselves. But it also moves beyond the grief towards many possible solutions. Women had to overcome *oppression*, but men's difficulties are with *isolation*. The enemies, the prisons from which men must escape, are:

- loneliness,
- compulsive competition, and
- lifelong emotional timidity.

Women's enemies were largely in the world around them. Men's enemies are often on the inside – in the walls we put up around our own hearts. The inner changes will have to come first before we can heal the world. Coming out from behind these walls (slowly, carefully) will mean that men can change and grow – to our own benefit and to the great benefit of women and children. Men's violence and greed will transform, as we become happier and healthier in our own spirits. The Men's Movement can deliver the changes that women and children have been waiting for.

Judging by the excitement, hope and relief I encounter on talkback radio, at public lectures and after my newspaper articles, many people are excited about this new way of looking at men's potentialities. Apart from the warmth and appreciation that men show for these ideas, there are other encouragements. Mothers of teenage sons come up to me with tears in their eyes – anxious and happy that something might really happen to improve their boys' self-esteem. Wives drag their husbands along. Single women, looking for a 'real man' to relate to, urge me to get a move on!

Men are a problem to women but rarely is this intentional. They are to an even greater degree a problem to themselves. The gender debate raged for twenty years, often fruitlessly, before we woke up to the fact that *men are not winners. There are very few happy men*. Men and women are co-victims in a pattern of living and relating that is in drastic need of revision. Simply blaming men doesn't change a thing. We need help to change ourselves. That is where the Men's Movement comes in.

Facing the facts

We are told it's a man's world, but the statistics on men's health, happiness and survival show this is a lie. Here are some of the *facts* about being a man in the late 20th century ...

- Men, on average, live for six years less than women do.
- Men routinely fail at close relationships. (Just two indicators: forty percent of marriages break down, and divorces are initiated by the woman in four out of five cases.)
- Over ninety percent of convicted acts of violence will be carried out by men, and seventy percent of the victims will be men.
- In school, around ninety percent of children with behaviour problems are boys and over eighty percent of children with learning problems are also boys.
- One in seven boys will experience sexual assault by an adult or older child before the age of eighteen.
- Men comprise over ninety percent of inmates of gaols. Men are also seventy-four percent of the unemployed.
- *The leading cause of death amongst men between twelve and sixty is self-inflicted death. In the 1993 ABS statistics, suicide accounted for one in every thirty-eight male deaths overall.*

Surely, it is the last point which most clearly shows we have a problem with men. Men and boys commit suicide four times more frequently than women. (The rate for men exceeds the road toll, though the two are probably blurred together. A 'single-vehicle accident' is often impossible to differentiate.)

My belief is that most men experience suicidal episodes and that many men are ambivalent about life. As a result they are really only half alive – stressed and neurotic. Consequently, we men have unique health problems – problems which point clearly to pressure, loneliness and stress as the causes. One study looked at the most common time of death for men and found that it was 9 a.m., on a Monday, from a heart attack. (Monday was also the most common day for men to suicide.) This is taking 'Mondayitis' too far!

By now, we're not talking about the extremes of male experience. This is getting close to you. (Or – if you are a woman – to your husband, your father, your sons.) We are talking about Everyman. The reality for most men in the Nineties is that *life is just not working.*

Enough negativity!! It's important to face how bad things have got – to roll around in it and feel the depth of it. There is 'nourishment in ashes'. You have to go down to go up. For most men, overcoming the 'I'm fine' habit (having been coached in shallow optimism for years) – *admitting you're stuffed* – is an important first step.

The men's movement

This book is about how we can change the lives of men. Many people now are beginning to rethink what it means to be a man. The Men's Movement is starting cautiously but is already a worldwide movement and shows a lot of energy and fire. So-called Sensitive New Age Guys were an improvement on macho-stupidity and violence, but they were also in danger of dying from self-flagellation. The Men's Movement is about positive, passionate masculinity – not paralysing self-doubt. There's a world of difference between caring for others from a feeling of self-worth and just being eager to please, as the 'feminist males' so clearly were doing. The Men's Movement is about *learning how to be confident and easy in making better marriages, jobs, pastimes, friendships and in developing a rich and sustaining inner life. It's about enjoying the key role of raising our sons and daughters to go further in the human adventure.*

Perhaps the core issue is *facing up to ourselves*, instead of running away or being self-destructive and hurtful to those around us.. Men are a practical gender – not given to prattling on. In the past there seemed no point in complaining, since nothing could be done. So for men, the shift had to come 'back to front'. Only with the possibility of change that the Men's Movement offers, can we finally admit how bad it really has been.

In this book

This is a practical book about what you, personally, can do to transform your life. It cites some of the best ideas from the Men's Movement around the world, draws on many personal experiences and is strongly flavoured by the thoughts and stories of men in my groups here in Australia. It is written for older men, young men, working men, unemployed men, businessmen, farmers, fathers, sons, gay men, married men, black, white and brown men; and, of course, for the women who love and want to understand men and see them find their spirit.

First up, you will get a chance to look at your 'personal masculine inheritance' – what you got and did not get from your father and the other men who raised you or failed to raise you. Then we'll journey through some very gutsy topics – sex and the male spirit, marriage and meeting women as equals, fatherhood, initiation, your job and your life, and spirituality – the deep parts of your experience – that give meaning to your life even when things are tough.

The book is broad, but by no means the last word – just a good kick-start.

Other voices

- The mass of men lead lives of quiet desperation

  Thoreau

- Who *taught* us to be a man? Nobody!

  Marvin Allen

- We are living at an important and fruitful moment now, for
  it is clear to men that the images of adult manhood given
  by popular culture are worn out; a man can no longer
  depend on them. By the time a man is thirty-five, he knows
  that the images of the right man, the tough man, the true
  man, which he received in high school, do not work in life.
  Such a man is open to new visions of what a man is or
  could be.

  Robert Bly

- Women were repressed by men for thousands of years.
  Finally men are getting a little repression – big deal! It's
  the 'repression we had to have'!

  Andrew Denton in 'The Great Debate'

- It is nothing like the women's movement, and probably
  never will be. Each man seems to be struggling with it
  quietly – at twenty-five, or thirty-five ... men are at the
  edge of a momentous change in their very identity as men,
  going beyond the change catalysed by the women's movement. It is a deceptively quiet movement, a shifting in
  direction, a saying 'no' to old patterns, a searching for new
  values, a struggling with basic questions that each man
  seems to be dealing with alone.

  Betty Friedan in *The Second Stage*

- Make no mistake about it: women want a men's movement. We are literally dying for it ... We have to use our instincts when deciding what to trust. We need to ask questions ... Then women can find allies in this struggle for a future that has never been.

    Gloria Steinem in *Women Respond to the Men's Movement*

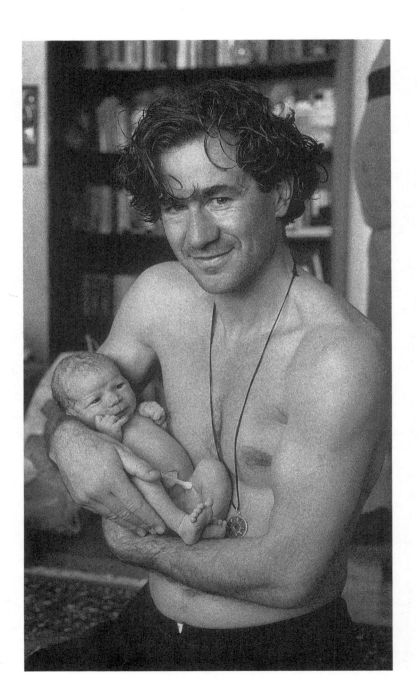

2
Seven Steps to Manhood

et's start with a simple question to you, as a man. Are you happy? Or are you just pretending to be and hoping that pretending will one day make it true? Do not answer this too quickly.

Left alone, a seedling will grow into a tree and a tadpole will turn into a frog. But a human child does not turn into a functioning adult without lots of help. To learn to be the gender you are, you probably need thousands of hours of interaction with older, more – mentally – equipped members *of your own gender*. In our society, girls get this contact from women on a day-to-day basis, but boys rarely get it from men. Women raise girls and boys – and most primary-school teachers are female. Most of the day, most of the time, men are usually not around. The result of this lack of male contact is a problem we are all aware of: that in today's world, little boys often just grow into **bigger** little boys. These emotional children in adult bodies then spend their lives pretending. The loneliness of this and the con-fusion – not knowing how to be comfortable with one's feelings or how to be close to others – just makes the pretending more compulsive and more isolating. *The lone-liness of men is something women rarely understand.*

Developing into a man

It takes the help of many men to turn a boy into a man. School doesn't do it. Watching TV doesn't do it. Mum, however hard she tries, can't do it on her own. Boys need exposure to healthy men, and this need continues into adult life. Young men need older men and middle-aged men still need even older men. If this need is met then life becomes vastly more bearable, secure, interesting and friendly. The sense of lonely struggle and imminent failure is replaced with an experience of life as a supported journey to mastery.

Look at this personally for a moment or two. If your developmental needs were not met in childhood and adolescence, you wouldn't necessarily know this. Even children growing up in the most bizarre families assume that their life is normal. You will only get a suspicion that things are amiss when your life starts to go wrong. This is what is happening to men today. Problems with health, marriage, parenthood, ability to make friends and failure at work are some of the ways they are alerted to the deep holes in their being. As young men we act cocky and cheerful but as the pressures of life stack up, our deficiencies become more obvious. The abysmal performance of our male leaders at all levels of society is a symptom of this problem. A male leader needs to draw on exceptional fathering experiences, since he is father to a team, an organisation or even a country.

In nature, all development follows a laid-down sequence. In a man's development, the sequence has been forgotten and the process largely left to chance. If we look at older cultures we see immense and focussed efforts going into the raising of boys – rituals, teachings and processes which have only feeble equivalents in our culture.

Robert Bly and others in the Men's Movement have identified a number of missing steps in men's development, which we'll soon explore. Perhaps these steps are the keys to really having a life as a man. The aim is not just to be well adjusted (!) but something more worthy – to have a glorious life. The Sioux hunter, the Zulu warrior, the Aboriginal elder and the medieval craftsman lived glorious lives and cared for and protected their people and their world. Why should modern man be any less a man than his ancestors?

Seven steps to manhood

Rather than unfold these gradually, let us 'hit you with them first up'. They may just touch a chord in you that gets you thinking. We can look at the details later. Here are the steps.

1 'Fixing it' with your father

Your father is your emotional line of contact to your masculinity. You have to work towards a clear and resolved relationship between yourself and him. *You cannot get on with your life successfully until you have understood him, forgiven him and come, in some way, to respect him.* You may do this in conversation with him if he's alive, or in your mind if he is now dead. Unless you do this work, his corpse will trip you up every time you make a move!

2 Finding sacredness in your sexuality

You have to find out how to be not just comfortable but transformed and fulfilled in your sexuality. Sex will either be a sleazy and obsessive part of your life or a sacred and powerful source of wellbeing. There isn't any in-between. First you must relocate your sexual energy in yourself, instead of giving it away to women. Then you need to learn the art of the chase – the specific role a man must take in the dance of male and female.

3 Meeting your partner on equal terms

Anyone can get a partner – the trick is keeping them. To do this you must learn how to meet your partner – and in fact all women – as a different but equal being. This means respecting her but respecting yourself too. In order to have

a successful marriage and one which lasts, you will sometimes need to be able to debate fiercely and to do so in a
safe and focussed way so that problems get solved. In a
modern marriage, soft men get left and bullies drive self-
respecting women away. Today's man has to learn to
communicate. A pretty radical idea!

4 Engaging actively with your kids

You can't parent from behind a newspaper and you can't
leave it all to your partner either – because a woman
doesn't have all the ingredients needed. You will have to
get the 'tough–tender' balance right with your children. This
is especially important for your sons, who will need many
hours a day of your care if they are to progress into
adulthood. Daughters too depend on you for a large slice
of their self-esteem.

5 Learning to have real male friends

You will have to get emotional support from other men and
find out how to complete your own initiation into manhood.
Also you must find some way to provide this for your
teenage sons. All men need the help of other men to
complete certain transitions, as well as just having a warm,
relaxed life.

6 Finding your heart in your work

You must find work you can believe in, so that the time
and energy of your working life is spent in a direction where
your heart lies. It isn't enough just to make a living. The
real work of men is to support and protect life and to build
towards a better world. If you don't believe in your own
work then the inner contradictions of it may start to slowly
kill you. This is a big one.

7 Freeing your wild spirit

The god of men does not dwell in the suburbs or the office
towers. Inner steadiness does not come from achievements
or possessions. You will need to find a spiritual basis for
your inner life that is specifically masculine and **based in**

nature, which connects you to the earth you live on. As you grow older this will be your source of strength and harmony, freeing you from fear and dependency on others.

That's the list. The sequence is not fixed. Some may be already accomplished in your life, others current and still others seemingly insurmountable. Some of these points may puzzle or surprise you, some may be striking a chord. By now you might be full of questions. If so, that's good. The whole of this book is devoted to exploring these ideas and to spelling out their practical implications. All of the above steps are necessary for you to progress to full manhood. So let's get started.

Other voices

- What is a man supposed to be ? What did you learn about how to be a man? From the audience, 'Big boys don't cry!' Big boys don't cry. The single most damaging thing you learn.

  Marvin Allen

- There's no sense in idealising pre-industrial culture, yet we know that today many fathers now work thirty or fifty miles from the house, and by the time they return at night the children are often in bed, and they themselves are too tired to do active fathering.

  Robert Bly

3
Liberation For the Rest of Us!

I'm watching late-night TV. It's 'The Clive James Show' and the guests are Germaine Greer and – wait for it – Billy Connolly! Germaine comes on first. She is her feisty self and, at the same time, unusually personal – sad even – about her life and the loneliness resulting from some of her choices. Then things lighten up. Billy Connolly is brought on and Clive James starts by asking him what he thinks of feminism. Billy answers, with much eye rolling and headshaking:

'Well, I don't know! I thought feminism just meant being nice to women! Giving them equal pay and all that! Sounds great! I'd hold the door open for New York women and be told "Fuuurrrrk Orrf!" Then I got feminism confused with sexism. I went to parties and said, "Well, I'm a sexist too!"

'I find the writings on it incredibly, ... uhh, boring. I tell my brain to read it and it just goes ... "Bye!" It was never the thing I was looking for, ... uh, feminism. It was never my holy grail!'

'It was never my holy grail!' That states the dilemma for men perfectly. Most men aged forty and under have lived their whole lives in the feminist era. Men over forty have usually had to come to terms with it too, in some shape or form. Not that this is yet a world where feminism has got its way, but it is a world where the attitudinal tide, the best opinion, the enlightened stance is in favour of women's worth, women's qualities and women's rights. This is great if you are a woman – but for even a well-intentioned man, well, it sort of puts you on the sidelines.

Feminism isn't for men

Billy Connolly's whole secret is his knack of saying the unsayable. (Germaine, of course, loved him – whereas she eats Sensitive New-Age Guys for breakfast.) This truth-telling role of comedians is important to our sanity. The unspeakable reality in this case is that feminism does nothing for men! It's not supposed to – except indirectly – by creating happier women.

Feminism is about women liberating themselves – changing perceptions, laws, employment practices and so on. It's wonderful – but as with black power, if you're white all you can do is accommodate it and cheer from the sidelines. It isn't a movement *for* you. (Woody Allen tells a story about majoring in Black Studies at Berkeley for three years. 'One more year to go', he says, 'and I'll be black!' But more of Woody Allen later.)

Feminism asks men to change, but it isn't *for* men. If you are a man, you can admire and support strong women, you can fight the abuse and oppression of vulnerable women, but you can't *be* a feminist because it isn't a club for you. You're still a lion with the vegetarians, and everyone knows it!

It's very important to understand the times you live in. Unseen forces carry us as we try to swim our own journey.

Feminism is easily the biggest movement in human history. Women across all cultures and religions have suffered immeasurably for thousands of years and now are catching up. If we include the struggle for women to have the vote in the early part of this century, then feminism is easily the most important thing to have happened in the 20th century.

Here is a single story among thousands of why we needed a women's movement. A woman friend of mine was deserted by her husband for another woman, in 1972. She had two young children and no income, so she applied for a pension. The Social Security office told her that to qualify, she had to be separated for six months and provide documented proof that she had not given her husband cause to leave. That is, she had to provide witnesses that she had (i) ironed his clothes, (ii) fed him proper meals and (iii) let him have sex!

All this changed in Australia with the Whitlam era and the Family Law Act, but it's very recent and should act as a reminder of why feminism was needed in the first place. Even today, less than ten percent of academic positions or senior management posts are held by women. Equality for women is still a distant dream.

Liberation's other half

Real gains **have** been made by women but the consensus in the Nineties is that things have bogged down or, worse, are going backwards. If this is true it isn't surprising – the reason is built-in. Put bluntly, *you can't liberate only half of the human race*. The idea of liberating women *from men* assumes that men were somehow the winners in a power struggle and that power was what life was all about. In short, feminism assumed that men were having a good time! Yet it's clear to anyone who thinks about it, that the sexist husband who beats his wife or the chauvinist boss who undermines and misuses women at work or the man who has sex with his children are hardly victorious or strong individuals. These kinds of men are usually pathetically insecure – hence their need to keep women down. They are 'on top' but hardly 'winners'. It's much more realistic to say that both men and women were trapped in a system which damaged them both. The way forward lies not in women fighting men but in women and men together fighting the ancient stupidities that have been bequeathed to them.

Consider the business and professional world as an example. For a lot of women, getting *equality* with men at work has gone badly astray. Those women who have learnt to compete on male terms – but then go on to live like men, talk like men, exploit like men – are the victims of this misunderstanding. They inherit ulcers, heart attacks and children who hate them. Welcome to the privileged world of men!

Because men are and always have been deeply frightened, they create a 'backlash' against women. When feminism is one-sided, it fuels just such a reaction. Violent men, for instance, (as we know from working with them in groups) are rarely angry below the surface bluster. Scared, yes; lonely, yes. Anger is only a cover. *Any move to change the order of things which does not also address the fact that men are equally lost, trapped and miserable, will only create its own resistance* – the much talked about 'backlash'.

The Men's Movement is not a backlash. Robert Bly, in the preface of *Iron John*, feels a need to state this very strongly:

> 'I want to make clear that this book does not seek to turn men against women, nor to return men to the domineering mode that has led to repression of women and their values for centuries. The thought of this book does not constitute a challenge to the women's movement. The two movements are related to each other, but each moves on a separate timetable.'

Bly is not blind to the problems that men create. He just differs as to the causes and the cure. Again, quoting from his preface:

'The dark side of men is clear. Their mad exploitation of earth resources, devaluation and humiliation of women, and obsession with tribal warfare [*Bosnia comes to mind*] are undeniable. Genetic inheritance contributes to their obsessions, but also culture and environment. We have defective mythologies that ignore masculine depth of feeling, ... teach obedience to the wrong powers, work to keep men boys, and entangle both men and women in systems of industrial domination that exclude both matriarchy and patriarchy.'

The needless argument about which gender is 'to blame' will come up constantly until we simply learn to drop it. Blaming men is neither compassionate, accurate or useful. Women who attack men as a group are simply passing on their own abuse. It may feel good, but it's inexcusable. The world already has enough hate. It needs more intelligence and it cries out for more goodwill.

What we must do now is to make comparable changes in the empowerment of men to those that have begun to happen for women. Most men (and certainly most able and thoughtful men) not only welcomed feminism – many of us grew up envying it, admiring it and working to further its aims. Therein lies the problem. If the most significant social movement of the time is one which does not involve you at all (and in fact excludes you by virtue of some dangly things between your legs), then you are in trouble! What are you supposed to do? The Men's Movement of the Nineties isn't a reaction to the Women's Movement. *It's the Women's Movement's missing half.*

Where men are going – an end to pretending

So what is the Men's Movement about? For a start it's about reaffirming that masculinity is a positive, life-supporting force – and working to bring this to the fore. Today in

Australia there are over 300 men's groups addressing this positive agenda. There has been a 'men's movement' of sorts for almost twenty years. Unfortunately, it was often based on apologising for being a man. Their intentions were honourable, and some positives have resulted. Everywhere today we see a greater emotional freedom in men (witness even our politicians and sportsmen showing their grief) and more affection amongst men. There is now much more widespread and outspoken disapproval of harassment and power plays by men over women. Yet the agenda and the energy of the 'male feminists' was often overwhelmingly negative, and most healthy men didn't want a bar of it. Imagine joining a movement or attending a group which started with the premise that you were born (and always would be) defective, second rate, by virtue of your sex. That you were intrinsically a rapist, child molester and murderer – and had better exercise some self-control! It was limited in its appeal!

As the idea leaked out, the ethos took shape in the mainstream as a caricature. The SNAG (Sensitive New Age Guy) was a figure of fun – not because he was sensitive but because he was transparent!

'If I have to act sensitive and warm and "help with" the housework and sleep in the wet patch to make it with these gorgeous feminist women, then what the heck!'

It smelled like an act and it usually was. From the Seventies onwards, 'pretend' SNAGS were everywhere. Worse still, the really concerned men were bogged down in self-apology and incapable of movement. (As if wearing a white ribbon would really stop rape or child sexual abuse. Hard work stops child abuse.) It's not possible to build a new identity on an inferiority complex. We had black pride, gay pride, women's pride – but men were supposed to start out with shame. By the early 1990s, the media was full of items about 'poor confused men'. It was time for a change.

People were forever talking about their 'role'. If you don't have a self, then you look for a 'role'. Men, you see, have played roles for a long time. As we said at the start of this book, men **pretend**. To get real, we have to dig down deeper.

Blame it on John Wayne!

Back thirty years ago, the role we played was well defined. It was the Fifties' Male. John Wayne probably epitomised the role best: Man as a block of wood!

Robert Bly describes the Fifties' man beautifully – his pluses and his minuses:

> 'He got to work early, laboured responsibly, supported his wife and children and admired discipline. Reagan is a sort of mummified version of this dogged type. This sort of man didn't see women's souls well, but he appreciated their bodies; and his view of culture ... was boyish and optimistic. Many of his qualities were strong and positive, but underneath the charm and bluff there was, and there remains, much isolation, deprivation and passivity. Unless he has an enemy, he isn't sure that he is alive.
>
> 'The Fifties' man was supposed to like football, be aggressive, stick up for the United States, never cry and always provide. But receptive space or intimate space was missing in this image of a man.'

Bly is describing our fathers' generation and also many of our own generation too. There is a lot of good in the Fifties' Male – loyalty, hard work, a willingness to do difficult things. When I've worked with Australian soldiers, engineers, foresters, the older style of policemen – you get this feeling. They know **how** to do a job, but not always why. This was the stuff that put men on the moon and men in Vietnam. How but not why. Action without feeling or, in the case of Vietnam, action first and feelings later.

Why was there this huge lack of feeling in our fathers' generation? Or, at least, why was there the struggle to keep feelings at bay, which made these men hold back from speaking much beyond an occasional grunt? The answer is obvious – because the Fifties' Man was also an act. He didn't know how to feel because feelings come from the inside. If your role model is wooden and remote, how can you learn to articulate what is happening on the inside? There is no data. He isn't saying things like, 'I'm feeling pretty unsupported here' or 'A man's gotta feel what a man's gotta feel'!

If a role model gives no information about the inner world, then the youngster following that model simply fails to develop an inner world. They still have feelings, but those feelings are chaotic and unmanageable because they have no names. So young men growing up all through this century learned to act. That's where we are caught today, between two acts – John Wayne (the he-man) and Woody Allen (the SNAG). A flip-flop of unreal, unworkable extremes.

(What has happened to Woody Allen is instructive. Under the surface of any SNAG, behind the niceness and meekness, are lusts and aggressions much more dangerous for being unacknowledged. In Allen's case, he stayed unashamed of a sexual relationship with a step-daughter less than half his age. His marriage exploded into wild recrimination and accusations of incest. In such a wonderfully creative man this was very sad. But, as the world was pretty much drawn to conclude, 'So much for the new age guy'.)

Deep masculinity

Phony toughness or phony niceness – that's where men were by the early Nineties. Small wonder men got confused. But there is a way through. There is such a thing as 'deep masculinity', which is latent in a young man and able to be developed and nurtured into its fullness. Rather than 'prove' you're a man, you take the steps that help you to *be* one based on latent abilities already inside you. Many rough-tough boys in early teens for example are wonderful with little children, if encouraged and coached.

Later, teenagers will work hard on a personal goal if somebody cares whether they achieve it. So masculine nurturing, and masculine persistence are developed. Masculinity has to be learned, from men who have learnt it from other men, and so on, back for aeons. Of course women can and do teach positive qualities to boys, but there are subtle and important differences in that how men teach, and in boys' willingness to learn. The Xervante people of the Brazilian rainforest have eight stages of manhood and spend forty years learning them. They produce perhaps the most balanced men on earth, straddling the qualities we seek – strong **and** tender, brave **and** compassionate. Xervante men are lovers of beauty and active in preserving it. Offered a life in the cities, the Xervante just laugh and go back to the forest. A Xervante man never feels alone. A Western man is on his own from teens onwards.

A new beginning

'A man needs other men – especially older men – to bless him, to honor him, to encourage him, to point out his mistakes and to raise his status.'

Douglas Gillette

The answer to masculine problems is crystal clear. We have to reforge a chain that was broken, by which men through the ages learned to be men. This is a recent problem, in the scale of things. It probably began about two hundred years ago, in the Industrial Revolution. We take industrialisation for granted now, yet its effects on us cannot be overstated. It was the biggest event in human history. It happened in one generation, two hundred years ago, for better or for worse – and we still live in its shadow. It started in English-speaking countries and has spread slowly across the globe. This is what we mean when we talk about 'developed' countries. They have passed through this total change of living.

The Industrial Revolution is usually seen in terms of what we gained – and we gained a great deal (or you would have just spent the day hoeing turnips in the rain!). But we have yet to take stock of what we lost. For the first time in half a million years of human existence, men stopped working alongside women and children in their villages and farms and went to work apart, in factories, and mines. And in a break with eternal tradition, boys began being raised by women. For aeons of time before this, boys grew up with the sweetness of male teaching from several older men who took pride and placed great store in their maturation. Unless the tribe or willage raised good men, everyone's life was endangered.

As late as 1900 in the U.S. (and probably Australia, too) over ninety percent of fathers were engaged in agriculture. In those days the son characteristically saw his father working at all times of the day and all seasons of the year.

The lack of male input to growing boys created a huge break in the family fabric, yet we adjusted to it and soon assumed it was normal. The possibility that boys might need fathering, for many hours a day, not just minutes – that uncles and grandfathers had a critical role in male mental health – was ignored. Deep and dangerous gaps in male development arose – perhaps even the seeds of the wars that plagued the modern world.

Father-hunger

Personal life was the most damaged. The 'Victorian' father emerged – alienated, remote, often violent, sexually disturbed in a variety of ways. As we modern men emerged from this – men born in the Thirties and Forties onwards – we mostly hated our fathers. But the hate was rooted in sorrow for the lost contact and love.

Men stumbled on, trying to invent themselves in a

vacuum. We were puzzled and blamed ourselves when this inevitably did not work. How could we grieve for what we didn't know we were missing? A simple, earthy term was coined to describe this hidden grief 'father-hunger'. Father-hunger is the deep biological need for strong, humorous, hairy, wild, tender, sweaty, caring, intelligent masculine input. For long satisfying hours spent learning to be confident and capable in the world, in the pleasure of doing and making, striving together and laughing at adversity, learning the joy of being a man from men who know these things and are willing to share them.

Father-hunger is perhaps the most important concept in male psychology. It's the starting point for most men in their own journey to health. How to recover what has been lost is the subject we'll address next.

In a nutshell

1 Feminism elevates women from a long subservience. It's important and must continue.

2 But most men have been subservient too – to a dehumanising system that only grew worse with the advent of the industrial era.

3 Today men are ripe for a transformation. Fathering is very likely the key place to start.

Other voices

- I like to think what I do is masculine ... when I hold a little baby and kiss it, that's the masculine part of me holding that little baby. When I have tears because I'm scared, or because I'm full of joy, they're all masculine. There's not a feminine thing about them.

  Marvin Allen

- When we walk into a contemporary house, it is often the mother who comes forward confidently. The father is somewhere else in the back, being inarticulate.

  Robert Bly

- The feminist critique of industrial society has put men on the defensive and masculinity itself on trial, as if there's something innately destructive in masculinity. The men's movement helps us reclaim and honour ... healthy masculinity, which includes its generative, earthy and nurturing qualities.

  Shepherd Bliss

- Some people make no distinction between the instinct for fierceness and the instinct for aggression. ... the separatist feminist movement, in a justified fear of brutality, has laboured to breed fierceness out of men.

  Robert Bly in *To Be a Man*

- This 'soft male' who makes a show of his 'false feminine' is easily detectable. He lacks potency in his voice, actions and being. And while he may love the planet and eat only vegetables, he lacks the ability to take firm action to save the planet or anyone or anything else. He lacks an energy that says 'yes' to life and 'no' to drugs, alcohol and other addictions and destructive behaviours.

John Lee in *At My Father's Wedding*

Male-Bashing

(This article, 'Male-Bashing' by Fredric Hayward, appears in *To Be a Man*.)

By far, male-bashing is the most popular topic in my current talk shows and interviews. Reporters and television crews have come to me from as far away as Denmark, Australia and Germany to investigate this American phenomenon. What is going on, they ask? Why do women want it? Why do men allow it?

The trend is particularly rampant in advertising. In a survey of a 1000 random advertisements, one hundred percent of the jerks singled out in male–female relationships were male. There were no exceptions. That is, whenever there was a husband–wife or boyfriend–girlfriend interaction, the one who was dumped on was the male.

One hundred percent of the ignorant ones were male. One hundred percent of the ones who lost a contest were male. One hundred percent of the ones who smelled bad were male. One hundred percent of the ones who were put down without retribution were male. Sometimes the male would insult the female, but she was always sure to get him back in spades before the commercial ended. One hundred percent of the objects of rejection were male. One hundred percent of the objects of anger were male. One hundred percent of the objects of violence were male.

In entertainment the trend is similarly raging. Some television shows are little more than a bunch of anti-male jokes strung together. Deciding to count the phenomenon during one episode of 'The Golden Girls', I found thirty-one women's insults of men compared to two men's insults of women. Family sitcoms like 'The Cosby Show' or 'Family Ties' have an unwritten rule that mothers are never to be the butt of jokes or made to look foolish.

As to literature, just glance through the recent bestseller lists. There is no anti-female literature that matches the anti-male tone of *Smart Women, Foolish Choices, Women Who Love Too Much, Men Who Can't Love, Men Who Hate Women and the Women Who Love Them*. Two authors told me about pressure from their editors to create anti-male titles as a way of increasing sales. The closest thing to a female flaw that one can publicly acknowledge is that women tend to 'love too much'.

Products also reflect the popularity of hating men. One owner of a greeting card store reported that male-bashing cards are her biggest selling line. 3M sells a variety of Post-it notes, such as 'The more I know about men the more I like my dog' and 'There are only two things wrong with men. Everything they say and everything they do'.

[*In Australia, the* All Men Are Bastards *calendars and diaries were big sellers. Imagine if the gender of these were reversed, what an uproar would have resulted.*]

Unfortunately, sexism teaches us to think of men as one giant organism that has been dominant for thousands of years, and that can handle (or even deserves) a generation or two of abuse. The reality is that men have the same insecurities as women, and the generation of abuse has already had dire consequences for male mental health. Boys, struggling with maturation and never knowing anything but the current age of abuse, suffer even more. [*Recall the suicide rates amongst young men being the leading cause of death – a clear indication of culturally low self-esteem.*] Relationships suffer as well. In male-bashing times, disagreements lead to the man feeling blamed and the woman feeling oppressed.

Since the dawn of history, the male–female relationship has been able to survive evolutionary traumas by remaining a perfectly balanced system. Both men and women had their sets of privileges and power. Both men and women had positive and negative stereotypes. Feminist activists were the first to recognise that the system was obsolete, but seem to be the last to recognise that the system was, at least, in balance. They disrupted the system, and that was good, but they disrupted the balance, and that was dangerous.

The current male-bashing trend appeals to the female consumer, upon whose whims our economy depends. It is comforting for women to think that men are always at fault, while women are always innocent. For society's sake, however, and for the health of future male–female relationships, we better start to curb the excesses of male bashing. It does not take many angry letters before an advertiser withdraws an offensive commercial or before a business-person changes an offensive product.

The alternative, allowing male-bashing to continue its momentum, can only lead to a men's movement as angry with women and far more violent than the women's movement has been towards men. It is time to speak out. It is time to recognise that male–female dynamics have been far more reciprocal than feminist theory portrays. To those who insist that the female perspective is the only perspective: Your day has come and gone.

4
You and Your Father

I would estimate that thirty per cent of men today don't speak to their father. Thirty per cent have a 'prickly' or hostile and difficult relationship. Thirty per cent go through the motions of being a good son – and discuss nothing deeper than lawnmowers. Less than ten percent of men are friends with their father and see them as a source of emotional support.'

Where are you at with *your* father?

and with older men in general? This is an important question – in fact your manhood depends on it. Manhood, it turns out, isn't an age or a stage – it's a connection. Unless you can connect to the inherited masculinity of generations of older men, you are as much use as a phone without a socket.

Think about this connection with your father for a moment. Your masculinity – unconsciously and whether you like it or not – is based on his. Most men realise (with alarm) that their father's mannerisms, stances and even words are deeply a part of them and likely to emerge at any time. If you are at war with him in your head, you are at war with masculinity itself. And so this often means you are hopelessly divided against yourself.

It's important at some stage of your life to have, if you possibly can organise it, a profound conversation with your father. Only by doing this can you get an understanding of his life, his reasons, his failures *and* his successes. Unless you do this, you will always be building your own manhood on shifting sands – on guesswork and childhood impressions which were never the whole story. Other older men and women may supplement what you didn't get from your father – in fact their role is vital – but his primary place in your life will still be there. Even if he was an alcoholic, a wife-beater, a child-abuser – even if you never met him – your biological father still matters. Until you come to terms with him *he will haunt you from the inside*, where he symbolically lives forever.

How your father colours your life

One of the ways that your father will 'hang around' is by colouring your attitude to all older men. Perhaps you don't trust older men – because you couldn't trust your father. Perhaps you are rebellious to authority in general because your father was unloving and harsh. Perhaps you try to impress older men because you couldn't please your father. Perhaps you have been feeling superior to older men, that you can do without them, or can put it over them. The fact is, until you reach a place where you can feel love and respect for your father and also *receive* the love and respect of older men, *you will remain a boy*.

I have spoken to men whose fathers died or abandoned their mothers and were never seen again. I've also talked to many men whose fathers committed suicide. This leads to deeply buried hurt and confusion, since the message a little child always takes is 'What did I do to make him leave? What's wrong with me?'

Men can suppress this pain by hard work and denial but will still be prone to outbursts of deep distress, often masked by anger. I've encouraged such men to make the journey into their father's past, which often means making a real-life journey interstate or overseas. It has lead men I've known to visit POW memorials in Europe, talking to contemporaries of their father, looking up long-lost relatives, making a deep personal journey to heal the emptiness and understand the whole picture and so let themselves and their fathers 'off the hook'. The journey can be into your own memory banks – as long forgotten incidents and experiences surface. Listening to other men's stories helps this, since our childhoods were so alike.

Sometimes dreams bring new information or just taking time to reflect.

This process is especially important if you are in a leadership role. You will never have authority until you can respect authority – which means, in this leaderless world, finding some authority worthy of your respect.

For those of us whose fathers are still alive, the situation is easier – somewhat. Many men will identify with the story of a man phoning his father, long distance. The younger man is making an attempt to bridge the gap that has grown between them. Father and son have had little contact in recent years and the son has been doing some thinking. When the father answers the phone, the son begins to try and tell him ...

> 'Hi, Dad, it's me.'
> 'Oh, uh huh! Hi, son! I'll go get your mother ...'
> 'No, don't get Mum. It's **you** I want to talk to ...'
> There's a pause ... then ...
> 'Why? Do you need money?'
> 'No, I don't need money.'
> And the younger man starts on his [somewhat rehearsed, but still vulnerable] speech ...
> 'I've just been remembering a lot about you, Dad, and the

things you did for me. Working all those years to put me through college, supporting us. My life is going well now and it's because of what you did to get me started. I just thought about it and realised I'd never really said 'Thanks ...'

Silence on the other end of the phone. The son continues.' ... I want to tell you ... Thanks. And that I love you.'

'You been drinking????'

Whenever I tell this story the audience laughs out loud, but the men laugh with eyes wet and shining.

What fathers wait to hear

Every father, however much he puts on a critical or indifferent exterior, will spend his life waiting at some deep level to know that his son loves **and** respects him. Make sure you absorb this point. *He will spend his life waiting.* This is the huge power that you hold in your hands, just by virtue of being a son. Everyone these days accepts that a parent has the power to crush a child's self-esteem. Few realise that a child, in time, holds the same power in reverse. Parents wait, however defensively, for their children to pass judgment. That's how life is.

A friend of mine had a father who was so impossible that he walked out of the house if ever somebody tried to talk to him about matters of importance. This old man got cancer (not surprisingly) and was dying now, with tubes in and out of him. My friend went in to the hospital, closed the door of his father's room and said, 'I've got you now!'. He began to tell him how angry he was and, also (after a time) what he appreciated about him. At the end they were holding hands.

At one stage in my life, I drove my father to a remote beach and refused to take him home until we talked! He came through very well!

So there is a responsibility here – and not just a duty. Getting this right will challenge you to the core. The words,

'I love you', are cheap and easily said, which is part of the reason we hesitate to speak them. It's not the words that matter. But the message is important, however it is conveyed. Whether it is through a tone of respect, a liking for each other's company, a hug or a touch, you will find your own way. Eventually though, to remove any doubt, you have to tell your father (and your mother) what you feel and all that you feel, or else just go on fudging it.

A lot is at stake. If you are a man and you do not confront this dragon, then your father will die hurting and a part of you will die as well. Bly claims that **'Many men go to their graves convinced that they have been an inadequate human being'**. They do this because of the lack of respect that has developed with those they love – not the least of these being their sons, their connection with eternal masculine life.

The pain of this cannot be overstated. It is possible that your father will seek you out one day to deal with this himself. It is possible but unlikely. You are the one who has the benefit of the insights of our generation. You are the one reading this book. You are the one who has grown bigger by standing on his shoulders.

Finding your father

You may have in-built prejudices against your father, for a surprising reason. Very often and sometimes with the best of intentions, a mother will turn her son against his father. Bly has a brief and powerful story (in 'A Gathering of Men') which, when he tells it, lands in an audience like an emotional hand grenade. It's about a man who decides to make up his own mind about his father:

> At about thirty-five, he began to wonder who his father really was. He hadn't seen his father in about ten years. He flew out to Seattle, where his father was living, knocked on the door and when his father opened the door, said, 'I want

you to understand one thing. I don't accept my mother's view of you any longer.'

What happened?

The father broke down into tears and said, 'Now I can die'.

Fathers wait. What else can they do?

If you're a father with an adult son (reading this book), then why wait? If you're a son with a living father, then Bly's challenge is clear. Are you ready to make that journey? Often, to start with, you don't feel much love for your father, much less respect him. Perhaps you hate him. If there are differences between you, then these cannot be ignored. **Don't pretend things are okay.** It simply won't work and you will feel cheapened. Differences have to be dealt with (more on this later).

> Some father-hungry sons embody a secret despair they do not even mention to women. Without actually investigating their own personal father, and why he is as he is, they fall into a fearful hopelessness, having fully accepted the generic diminished idea of father. I am the son of defective male material, and I'll probably be the same as he is.
>
> Robert Bly

Finding an understanding of their father's position is a necessary work for all sons, if they are ever to graduate as men. **Respect (love mixed with admiration) is the food of the male soul.** Sons have to 'discover' respect *for* their fathers, which is not the same as pretending it. They also need to receive respect *from* their fathers.

The approval all sons crave

In a superb book for Christians on men's development, called *Healing the Masculine Soul*, Gordon Dalbey, a minister, tells a complementary story to the phone-call story at the start of this chapter. This time the son is waiting to hear that his father loves/respects/admires him back.

The young man, in his late twenties, writes to his father. The young man is a successful professional, but plagued with insecurities. In the letter he writes, he is direct and to the point. He asks his father whether he loves him. A letter comes back in reply: 'I love all my kids – you should know that'.

Can you spot the deliberate error? The old bugger still hasn't said it. You see?

The young man feels let down, though it takes a while to work out why. He eventually realises he's been short-changed and **this was what always happened**, throughout his childhood. 'I love all my kids ...' A clear statement is deferred, implied. Direct praise is avoided. Direct contact is never made. Encouraged by Dalbey, the son persisted. He wrote another letter. He was frightened to do so, but he wrote anyway. Here are the exact words of the father's reply:

> I have to thank you for pushing me with your question. I guess I hadn't really thought that deeply about it. But when I did think about it, I realised that I do love you, Peter, and I need to say that for myself probably as much as you may need to hear it.

Nothing is more powerful in the psychology of childhood than the need for love and approval. Unless a child receives clear and tangible demonstrations of these, then he or she will wither like a flower without water. It's as basic as that. I've watched tiny children in hovels in Calcutta dancing for their family and friends, who respond with warm applause and hugs. I've also watched Australian children bring home their report cards from their expensive private school, young faces eager for praise, only to receive cool, critical appraisals from their performance-oriented, uptight parents.

I don't in my heart understand where this parental coldness comes from. When I look at my own kids through certain eyes, the urge to hug them and praise them to the skies is sometimes overwhelming – not because they are any different to any other child (or just because they are 'mine') but because they are young human beings and glorious. Something must go badly wrong for parents to shut down these natural feelings.

What is the result of lack of closeness with the father? If love is what we hunger for and it is not forthcoming, then a warp in our life sets in. When our natural need for love is fulfilled, it settles into the background and we can get on with our life. Unfulfilled, the need for approval drives us like an obsession. Many of the people who dominate our media – business tycoons, politicians and obsessive sports achievers – are mostly driven by this unfulfilled hunger. *'See, Dad? See what I can do?'* And of course it doesn't work. *'But, son, can't you do better?'*

Whilst it is always somewhat difficult for men of differing generations to reconcile with one another, consider the problems raised if there is a major difference of orientation – for instance, the situation of a gay son (or a gay father for that matter). At heart the issue is really the same: Do you love me, even though I differ from what you expect? I am not the one you dreamed of. The wonderful film, *The Sum of Us*, with Jack Thompson and Russell Crowe, is great watching for any father, especially those with gay offspring.

Many wounds arise at this time from fathers who wanted a son and got a daughter, wanted an athlete and got an artist, wanted a musician and got a labourer; wanted gold medals and got cerebral palsy.

It might be one of the biggest stretches for our souls on this earth – to abandon our shallow egotistical dreams and to realise how much better our real children are than any dream could be. To honour the grief, feel it, explore it, and let it pass.

Fixing it with your father

Clearly, things are best worked out between living fathers and sons. Once you accept this as a necessary step in your own liberation, it comes down to practicalities. Men I talk with often say they are afraid of starting any real discussion with their fathers, for fear of starting a huge fight. Perhaps many fathers also live in fear that their sons will show up armed with sacks full of blame and criticism of their inadequacy. They are hardly likely to expect a good outcome.

One way is to go in with an open mind. Don't start with your fists up. ('Justify yourself, you old bastard!') Wait for the right time. When the evening is warm and the beer is cold and there are no women around. Ask him for the true story about his life and how it was for him during your childhood. Ask him about his work, his life and the decisions he made. Be non-judgmental. (If you find it hard to be this way, remember your son will weigh you on these same scales too.)

Go back further still. Find out what was going on in your father's childhood. Then move on to when he was raising you. The truth – his truth – will often be quite different to your childhood impressions. You are humanising your father in your own mind by doing this, filling out the picture, letting him off the hook of the role all children cast their parents in.

Some fathers will be totally evasive – walking from the room, refusing point blank to speak. I've known fist fights to develop, but I don't recommend this! Remember the goal – you are breaking down **the defences**, not the man.

The aim is to get the story straight. What really was going on all those years ago? Be prepared for surprises.

A friend of mine, Trevor (now in his early fifties), gave this example. When he was a boy, his father would take him on a paper round by car, each morning. They spent about two hours together each day in a peaceful rhythm of teamwork, as the sun slowly came up and melted the frost. It was his favourite time of the day; he loved the closeness to his father and the feeling of being useful in a man's world. Then one day, his father was offered a chance to leave his day job (which he hated) and be a partner in the newsagency that owned the paper round. To his son's dismay, he turned it down. The newsagency business was sold and the paper round ended.

Trevor stayed angry about this for about thirty years. 'He doesn't want to be with me!' When his dad got old and sick, he asked him about it.

'How come you didn't buy into the newsagency and keep up the paper round?'

'Because the partner was a gambler and we would have all gone broke.'

Simple as that.

Becoming a parent yourself cannot be beaten as a way to gain compassion for your own parents. A man in one of my groups, Mark, supported his wife through a 'cancer scare' which lasted about four years. At times he would be very uptight and scared and he would often react angrily to his young son, who was just being a normal demanding kid, unaware of the situation. Mark was not yet ready to tell his son about his worries and the eight-year-old was living in an unknown space – a kind of emotional minefield.

Eventually when his son was twelve, Mark joined a men's group. The other men urged him to explain what had happened. His son – who earlier would have perhaps been very worried – was relieved to understand, and proud to be trusted. His behaviour and school work both improved. Children often do not know what is going on, and we don't always make the right judgment about when to involve them and when not to. *They may just make the conclusion we don't like them and keep that conclusion for life.*

These are important things to clear up. As **you** talk to **your** father, you may find that things fall into place. One of the biggest things is to simply say, 'Thanks'. There may be many specific memories or instances which you recall as a beautiful part of your growing up. He may have no idea that he ever 'got it right'.

On the other hand, appreciation may be the last thing

you feel. If you are primarily angry about your childhood, begin (carefully) to say so. Tell him what you hated, what you found terrifying or how lonely and sad you felt through his lack of appreciation and warmth. He may rail back at you. He may just criticise you all over again. Don't give up – you are not a child now. Stay clear-headed. Ask why. Ask to know everything. Eventually, some understanding – some forgiveness, perhaps apology or some perspective – will enter into the air between you. No-one can predict or program how this will happen. Prepare to be surprised.

One of the few definites that has emerged in 20th century psychology is that unfinished business has to be finished. It isn't enough to 'forgive and forget' – to say that 'they had it tough' or 'they were only doing their best' or 'they're old now – why make waves?'. This doesn't address the truth nor does it address the inner child in you who has real hurt that needs to be assuaged. Short-cutting this work patronises your father and alienates you. You just get more distant.

Remember that the goal is to **get things right between you**. You are not there to get even, to 'make him suffer like he made me suffer' or anything like that. That would just spin the wheels of pain around one more time. You are aiming for a resolution which is real and complete. You want to heal both of you.

Loving your father in yourself

Most men find talking about their father an uncomfortable subject, and in fact men have succeeded in avoiding it for many generations. This is a pity because in doing so they cut their own roots. Therapeutic lore tells us we have to make peace with our parents, but ancient tradition takes a less compromising approach. In a sense, you **are** your father. You are an individual only to the extent that you build your own structure on top of what he has given you. Deep down inside you stand on all kinds of foundations which you must get to know, allow for and understand. Most of us have discovered, uneasily, that we have gestures, mannerisms or ways of doing things that are exactly those of our father. The answer isn't to try and eradicate them. The psyche throws nothing away. You have to learn to love 'your father in you'. If you don't deal with this, then you will very often be at war with yourself.

How many men do you know who are like this? As they split the wood or fix the car, or write a cheque, you can almost hear them muttering in argument with a long-dead ghost: 'You're making a mess of that, son!' 'Fuck off, Dad!' Forgiving your father – not just by effort of will but by actual factual understanding of his life – will be one of the most freeing things you ever do.

Some men get very sad at this point – because their father is already dead, and the conversations we are suggesting can never take place. It seems that an opportunity has been lost forever. Not true. He is *in* you and you can begin the process. In imagination, in dreaming, by talking to his grave or writing him a letter, you can begin to shift the grief. It is awkward but important. You can go on an actual, personal odyssey – finding out more information, travelling to his place of birth and the locations of significant events in his life. Or by talking to his contemporaries, start to fill in the missing details. Very often, it helps you to discuss this quest with other men on similar journeys. We all have so much in common and can help each other's grief to release; finding support and clarification at the same time. A surprising amount of feeling flows out with this process and much health and strength flows in to take its place.

Don't run from the past; it is always, eventually, a treasure trove.

In a nutshell

1 Your father is the person who first and most power-
fully 'taught' you what manhood means. He did this
by just being your father. Like it or not, he is in
your head and in your sinews and nerves forever.

2 This fatherly 'inheritance' is a mixture of utter garbage and priceless treasure. Unless you get in and
sort it out, you will never know which is which. Most
men stay out of the 'attic', the part of their mind
where this is all stored. They decide it is all junk, but
leave it right where it is – unexamined. As a result, a
funny smell is always drifting down and tainting their
lives. At the same time they feel deprived – missing
out on the jewels and riches concealed in the heap.

3 By far the easiest way to sort the heap is to have a
certain kind of conversation or series of conversations
with your father. Find out from him:
a. The truth about *your* childhood.
What was happening for him, when you were
conceived, born and were growing up? This will shed
much new light on what was going on, perceived by
you only through a child's eyes at the time.
b. The truth about *his* childhood.
What was the story of his childhood and young
manhood? What did *he* bring to bear on his raising of
you?

4 These conversations will be a two-way exchange of
gifts, as you tell him your experience and ask him
questions about his. Be prepared for surprises. Don't
be fobbed off with comfortable replies, clichés or

skimming over things. You are after the real blood, sweat and tears of his life and yours.

5 If your father is dead, then you might have to 'dig him up'. Here are some ways:

- Write a letter to him as if he were alive.
- Visit the significant places in his life.
- Talk to others who might know more about him.
- Decide to dream about him.
- Talk with a male counsellor about him, in order to reactivate your feelings and recollections.

Good luck, and courage.

Other voices

- We were not like father and son, my father sometimes said, we were like buddies. I think my father actually believed this. I never did. I did not want to be his buddy; I wanted to be his son. What passed between us as masculine banter exhausted and appalled me.

  James Baldwin

- We can overload our male-longings onto our fathers. We need to also remember that the loss of men's lodges, the company of uncles, grandfathers and the lost mythology and heritage of being a man, go much wider than this. In no traditional society was the training of young boys left in the hands of the father alone. The entire male community participated in this important work. Our father didn't have these connections either – he was as lost as we are.

  Robert Bly in *Wingspan*

- I do not want my children to have a monolithic memory of me. ... On the contrary, I would like them to know the vulnerable man that I am, as vulnerable as they and perhaps more so.

  Georges Simenon

- Both Freud and Jung were mothers' men, and our psychology comes out of them.

  Robert Bly in *Wingspan*

- Not all men missed out. Some tell stories of generous supporting fathers, who praised, loved and protected them as best they could, and even initiated them as best they could ...

  Robert Bly in *Wingspan*

• My father never stood up to my mother, and I'm still angry about that.

John Lee in *At My Father's Wedding*

• There's a lot of talk about physically and/or emotionally absent dads, but sons are also beginning to ask themselves, 'Was my father really absent, or did he and I unconsciously conspire to ignore each other?'

Christopher Harding in *Wingspan*

• Many young Hollywood writers, rather than confront their fathers in Kansas, take revenge on the remote father by making all adult men look like fools. They attack the respect for masculine integrity that every father, underneath, wants to pass on to his grandchildren and great-grandchildren.

Robert Bly

5
Sex and Spirit

What should be one of our greatest glories in life is often one of the greatest disappointments. Deep down many men feel themselves to be 'creeps'. I would estimate that sixty percent of men under forty are sex-addicted as opposed to sexual in a whole and balanced way.

When it comes to sex, men have been badly short-changed. Human sexuality is potentially a huge energy source which pushes us towards union with a partner and release from the ordinary. It's tragic that a facet of life so important to us has been exploited, misunderstood and demeaned by our culture and our religion. Most men are basically still ashamed of their sexual feelings. At best we have been taught to see our sexuality as something *ordinary* – just an itch to be scratched. We come through boyhood into manhood having all kinds of cheapened messages about our deepest feelings. 'Slugs and snails and puppy dogs' tails' is not a great beginning – and it's all downhill from there. Our penises should be winged steeds on which to fly to heaven. Instead they just get used to nail us to the ground.

Men's sexuality urgently needs to be made richer in pleasure and in meaning. The changes that the Men's

Movement are creating are as significant as the freeing-up of women's sexuality that took place in the Sixties through feminism. Women, you'll recall, had to discover *themselves* first, then educate men in how to pleasure them. Likewise, men have to talk and understand themselves, exploring what they want from sex and what they don't want, at the same time refusing to be demeaned or be self-demeaning. This self-exploration will give what has always been missing from our sex lives – the confidence to be able to talk honestly and easily about sex to our partners, and to have more exuberant and intimate lovemaking as a result.

Are most men non-orgasmic?

Male sexuality, especially the nature of the male climax, is grossly misunderstood by men – and women. Columnist Michael Ventura wrote this brilliant analysis:

> ... certainly the weakest, silliest aspect of feminism – which for the most part has been an overwhelmingly beneficial movement – has been its description of male sexuality. It was a description that assumed a monolithic mono-intentional erection; it was a description that equated the ejaculation of sperm with coming. But there are many secret passageways within an erection. As far as the question of male coming – it is an immense and untried question. Ejaculation is a muscle spasm that many men often feel with virtually no sensation but the twitch of the spasm. To ejaculate is not necessarily to come. *Coming involves a constellation of sensations, physical, psychic, emotional, of virtually infinite shadings.* Coming may *sometimes* or *often* occur at the moment of ejaculation, when it occurs at all. *But many ejaculations for many men happen without any sensation of coming.*
>
> Until a woman understands this she doesn't know that first thing about male sexuality. Nor do many men. There is ample evidence in face after face that, as there are women

who have never come, so there are **men who have often
ejaculated but never come.** And they likely don't know it,
as many women never knew it until a few began to be vocal
about such things. These men live in terrifying and baffling
sexual numbness in which they try the right moves and say
the right things but every climax is, literally, an anticlimax.
It is no wonder that in time they have less and less connection with their own bodies, and are increasingly distant from
the women they want to love.

(From *To Be a Man*, edited by K. Thompson)

This takes some digesting. There are, it seems orgasms and
orgasms. Norman Mailer wrote of the difference between
'orgasms stunted as lives, screwed as mean and fierce and
squashed and cramped as the lives of men and women
whose history was daily torture' and contrasts these with
others 'as far away as the aria and the hunt and the devil's
ice of a dive, orgasms like the collision of a truck or coming
as soft as snow, arriving with the riches of a king in
costume or slipping in the sneaky heat of a slide down
slippery slopes'. (From *The Prisoner of Sex*)

This represents a delightful variety. (Although there is
little mention of closeness, contact or any other emotional
qualities in Mailer's writings. He's still hung up on sensation
not emotion. It's him and his body, with some woman along
for the ride!)

An earlier book I wrote with Shaaron Biddulph, *The
Making of Love*, describes the deep connection that is the
real goal of lovemaking – looking soft-eyed into one another's faces, hearts open, bodies relaxed and abandoned,
gradually letting go of all defences in trust of each other
and of the natural power that possesses you. In short, 'Once
you have **made love**, then just having sex will never do'.

This isn't to say that lovemaking always has to be so
intense, but that it is a whole-person thing – not just (to
use Carl Whitaker's phrase), 'a penis and a vagina going
out on a date together'!

Loving as a whole man

The popular term for sexual climax, 'coming', is such an interesting choice of word. Who is it that is arriving? Clearly the divinity in the man is arriving. The everyday sense of self is awed and overtaken by this feeling of being something bigger and better – the truth really, since our everyday sense of self is not the whole story. In lovemaking, the god in man meets the goddess in woman and they are spun through cosmic space and time, knowing everything, lost in love. Regaining this sense of spirit in one's sexual life takes application. It can be as simple and as profound as just learning to relax.

John O'Hara, in his novel *Appointment in Samarra*, has one of his characters express it this way:

> I never made love before, I just screwed. But when it happened, it was like nothing I'd ever experienced before. I think I must have blacked out for a second and all I was aware of was some kind of incredible warmth, my whole body was filled with it and I didn't want to leave her or roll away from her. I wanted to get closer to her, very close. I could feel the warmth of her body against mine, soft and gentle and for the first time in my life I stayed in a woman's arms and fell asleep.

Paul Olson (in *Wingspan*) comments on this passage: 'What he does with that experience only time will tell. He can deny it in the morning. Or he can enter it fully and never again feel the need to run away.'

Clearly for us to experience this kind of union (what some might call 'sacred sex') requires all kinds of readiness, timing, openness and communication – as well as just good luck! A lot of other things have to be right. It may require years of gradually opening the body, learning to trust and becoming natural. Yet these years would be clearly well spent. We start life as tender babies and spend our whole life just regaining that absolute openness and trust.

An important ingredient for total lovemaking is the inclusion of nature – of letting in the signals and rhythms that the natural world sends to our cells to tune them in. That's what romance means – it means not artificial. Even in terms like 'the romance of sail' we are noticing a preference for the natural elements over the man-made environment. The old cliches endure because they are potent triggers. We think of romance as standing on an ocean beach watching the moon rise, of dining by candlelight, making love on a rug by a fireside or impulsively falling to the ground together in the long grass, laughing and pulling off each other's clothes to explore the warm skin beneath. Sex is about going back to nature, giving way to wildness – something you should never get too old for! Romance means bringing a wild heart to an erotic body, 'With the naked earth beneath us and the universe above'.

Men and whole-body sex

Feminism gave women back the power to control their own bodies – and the pleasure of fully being alive to their bodies. Women today can decide for themselves whether and when they want sex and how they want it to be. In the daring first studies of the Fifties and earlier, fewer than twenty percent of women were found to be orgasmic. Learning to become so, and to confidently and routinely let their partners know their needs and desires, was a very major shift – no less important because it took place in the privacy of a million bedrooms.

Like the women of the Victorian era, most men don't know what they are missing. One only has to watch the reptilian grunting and grinding of the men in 'adult' movies to realize these guys have never seen or had a real orgasm. Many men, too, need to become orgasmic – as opposed to just ejaculatory. One way to start is by placing less emphasis on the mechanical outer performance or actions, and more on the inner qualities of sensory and emotional experience. We men feel pretty lucky if our partner asks what we would like to *do* in bed. But the most magical woman is the one who asks what we would like to *feel*.

Barry Oakley pointed this out in his column in the *Australian Magazine* – using two contrasting quotations. The first is by Ken Follett, from his blockbuster, *Night Over Water*:

> This was not what was supposed to happen, she thought weakly. He pushed her gently backwards on the bed and her hat fell off. "This isn't right", she said feebly. He kissed her mouth, nibbling her lips gently with his own. She felt his fingers through the fine silk of her panties ...

You'll notice straight away that it's all action and adverbs. There is nothing about feeling or inner experience. The passage is mechanical and totally devoid of charm.

Then, for comparison, Oakley quotes D.H. Lawrence, from *Women in Love*:

> 'She was with Birkin, she had just come into life, here in the high snow, against the stars. What had she to do with parents and antecedents? She knew herself new and unbegotten, she had no father, no mother, no anterior connections, she was herself pure and silvery, she belonged only to the oneness with Birkin, a oneness that struck deeper notes, sounding into the heart of the universe, the heart of reality, where she had never existed before.'

It works from the inside out – from the real experience. Only great writers can do this, for a simple reason: you had to have been there.

The Lawrence quote tells nothing at all about the details. Nothing for little boys to giggle about, since they would simply not understand. These days we inform kids about the mechanics of sex – in the modern world this is a necessity. But in a sense we cannot tell them anything of what sex is really about. These skills and perceptions, one way or another, have to be taught or at least nurtured and encouraged. The beginnings of sexual experience are largely private. We begin by understanding ourselves and move outwards.

Self-love

Sex therapists and educators encourage masturbation as an important part of learning and maintaining healthy sexuality. In a man's life, self-pleasuring begins in the early teens, long before we establish relationships with women. It occurs surprisingly often (according to recent studies) during those relationships and will probably continue afterwards. It's a long-term project!

For men willing to utilise their imagination and capacities for fantasy, masturbation is an exercise in sexual independence and in practising sensuousness. It needs to be – from the accounts of many women, the majority of men need all the practice they can get! By not rushing, by experimenting, we become more skilful and sensuous lovers. (It was the furtiveness and hurry of teenage masturbation that has led to the widepread premature ejaculation problems in adults.) By having a playful and happy approach to self-pleasuring, men and their lovers benefit enormously.

For men of any age, the aim in self-stimulation is to create a sense of specialness and atmosphere. In recent decades, masturbation stopped being a mortal sin, but it only moved one notch away – to being a kind of necessary evil. It was permitted – but only to 'blow off' excess sexual steam! (One suspects it was probably more fun when it was a sin!)

It's important to be leisurely, relaxed, unhurried and tuned-in to the head-to-toe sensations of arousal – to be more open to the pleasures of before and after. Self-pleasuring – for both men and women – is a kind of apprenticeship. It's an important source of self-awareness – a prerequisite to being good in bed. It's here that we learn what we like, so that we can communicate this to our partner. It's here that we learn to let ourselves be totally receptive (a difficult thing for many men) – surrendering, allowing one's whole body to receive the loving energy that becomes freely available in sexual exchange.

Keeping the magic

Our bodies give us the message from inside: sex is magic! But from the outside – from magazines, playground humour and perhaps the sexual abuse they received from older men or women – boys and young men get a sleazy, animal, dirty image of their sexual yearnings. As fathers and mothers we have to work hard to strengthen the positive – and fend off the negative messages bombarding our sons. As adult men we have to remind ourselves often that our sexuality, as it is, is wholesome and good.

Late one night I heard a radio interview with the publishers of a weekly picture magazine. It was the kind of magazine that has huge boobs pointing out from the cover every week and stories like 'Man Bonks Shark' (or vice versa) on the inside. The magazine editors joked about the whole culture of the magazine, the stories they got away with – and what the readers will tolerate. 'U.S. Warship Found on the Moon' was one of them.

Listening to the interview, I often found myself smiling – but good humour walks a fine edge. The reason for the interview was widespread criticism of a recent cover photograph showing a naked woman wearing a dog chain, which had prompted some new legislation. Most people, rightly, found this cover offensive. The interview ended with the predictable question: 'Does your magazine cheapen women?'

'No, not really,' the editor answered. But then he went on, laughing, 'If it demeans anyone, it's the blokes who read it!' Precisely.

When women's bodies are used (and when women allow their bodies to be used) to sell commodities, then everyone is misused. Even the models and photographers need to be mindful that, with the frequency of child sexual abuse, when they promise and don't deliver, it is often a little child who pays out.

Finding a balance

Parents in Victorian times wanted to keep their children ignorant of sex forever. Sexual information has made a happier, more sane and honest world, freer of the perversions and cruelties that ran thickly under the veneer of Victorian propriety.

Today's parents don't object to information – it's misinformation that angers us. We want our children to be fully switched-on to sexuality. We want this to happen, though, in a timely way, keyed to their level of growth and maturity. Many experts have noted that exposure of children to the media robs them of their childhood – it disempowers, frightens and overwhelms.

A child's innocence can be stolen by an abuser, but it can be knocked around badly by an ill-timed video too. We have to be careful, and the media need to fix up their act or face a growing parent boycott.

We need erotica, but why is it often so bad – almost demoralising? We need some way (as the Japanese once used their 'pillow books') to convey to our kids what is really going on inside two people in love. Poetry maybe. Sex education teaches us the plumbing – it's necessary, but drab. Love education might be a little more challenging.

In their book *Raising A Son,* Don and Jeanne Elium describe a celebration they spent with each of their sons at around the age of ten, in which they recapped not just the 'facts' of life, but also the 'feeling' – sharing the specialness and intensity of what sex meant to them in their marriage. They then took their son out on a special meal in a 'grown up' restaurant, to honour his approach to adolescence. Censorship is too passive a response – somehow we have to be counter-attacking – immunising our young men with more powerful magic than the lowest common-denominator views of sex as cheap relief.

The 'creepification' of men's sexuality

Cheapening isn't the only risk. There is a deeper danger for boys and men in the power of sex. If this much energy doesn't flow in a good direction, it can sometimes go in a very bad one. There is a major and justified focus in feminism on the capacity of men to hurt and harm in the sexual arena – to exploit, harass, rape and kill. This isn't a peripheral concern – child sexual abuse, to choose just one example, occurs in virtually every street in the country. 'All men are animals' isn't an explanation or a cure for this. We urgently have to explore male sexual development, to find out how a healthy energy can become so badly misdirected.

The following was written by Jai Noa, a physically disabled man, who, in his crippled state, observed that he was quickly turning into a *creep*. He then made an astonishing leap from examining his own condition, to noticing that in our society this process happens to *all* men to some extent. Almost all of us feel romantically crippled at some time. Given the media messages mentioned above – the look-but-don't-touch culture – we can easily start to see our sexuality as loathsome and so begin to incubate a desire to make women suffer in 'revenge'. In Noa's own words:

> I use the idiom 'creep' in a very special sense. 'Creep' refers to the ashamed sexuality of most men, which is an inescapable fact of our social life and one which each of us must confront sooner or later. It is ironic that if there is an almost universal manner in which men share a common crippledness, it is in the realm of sexual expression ...
>
> A creature of low self-esteem, the creep feels he cannot develop sustained intimate friendships with others. Despair-

ing of the intersubjective happiness, he takes the other,
[the woman] as an object to exploit as best he can. This is
a cynical attempt to validate himself through domination.
The delightful joys of erotic pleasure are turned into their
opposite by a guilt-ridden quest for power. The creep then
is a voyeur, a pornophile and an exhibitionist. He enjoys
not only invading the sexual space of others, but also a feeling that his penis has the power to cause a reaction, even
if only one of discomfort or disgust.

The heterosexual male creep tries to reduce all women to
whores, i.e. to what he thinks of as dirty sluts, who are so
low they would fuck someone as contemptible as himself
(and thereby elevate him!). He may cruise bars or parties in
search of a drunken easy lay. In his masturbation fantasies
he chooses a woman who is too good for him and envisions
her as a slave of sexual passion.

The creep is a man who fails to live up to the romantic
ideal and who feels crushed, bitter and resigned to this failure. And since most men suffer defeat in the romantic
meritocracy, at one time or another, the cripple can find his
identity partially located in the world of men. Increasingly,
during his teenage years and for an indefinite period of
time thereafter, the cripple can find a bond with any men
who indulge in misogyny.

There is nothing crippled about this man's grasp of language! When I first read this essay, 'The Cripple and the
Man', I sat for a long time in silence! It's possible that Noa
has answered one of the social problems of our time. Let's
just pull out a key sentence: 'Despairing of intersubjective
happiness, he takes others as an object to exploit as best
he can'. In other words, despairing of ever winning anyone's love and closeness, the man who becomes a creep
prefers to have the upper hand. Here we have laid open
before us the rapist, the child molester, the pornography
addict, the serial killer and the wife beater. We also have
Everyman, struggling to feel okay about his wants and

desires in a seeming 'one-down' position with women – knowing well the feelings expressed in the Dr Hook song, 'Girls can get it any time they want'!

This is more than just a problem of *sexual* confidence. Many men confuse sexual rejection with outright rejection – of themselves, and their lovability – so feel double the pain. (It may spread to other aspects of their performance – their earning capacity, physique and so on.)

All human beings need to feel loved. To be valued *as we are*, treated with kindness and to experience daily intimacy. Since most men come to women with such a deep lack of inner worth, they will be tempted – instead of risking rejection as an equal – to use their strength, their sneakiness, their money and other power plays to impose their needs. Women pay a great price for this. It's a double tragedy. The whole of the prostitution industry relies on the emotional impoverishment of men – so many of whom feel more comfortable buying 'pretend' love than dealing with the complexities of the real thing.

Sexual-abuse perpetrators

For most men, their perceived lack of sexual power is just depressing. But for men who have been badly abused by their mothers or fathers, and taken into their being the 'hurt-or be-hurt' ethos, it becomes more dangerous. 'If you can't get love, get even', becomes this person's inner dynamic.

The rapist knows his victim is helpless and derives pleasure from this. The child molester can only feel good in a position of total power and control. He feels safer this way. Why risk rejection from an adult when you can control a child? There are other complicating factors: often aggression and arousal have been mislinked by the unfortunate training ground of his childhood. Some abusers soothe the memory of the abuse in their own childhood by switching the roles around. It isn't possible to think about these things without one's skin beginning to crawl, but for the sake of women and children everywhere we have to face them. It's known that one in six children in our society are sexually abused at some time, usually by a man who is part of their family or social circle. In the course of his career, an abusive man may have access to dozens of children, grandchildren, friends, cousins. The damage to the emotional wellbeing of these children – unless concerted healing intervention takes place – is life-long. Suicide, anorexia, alcoholism, marital problems, drug addiction, depression, abusiveness to one's own children, are just a few of the symptoms.

The violation these men commit is inexcusable; but starts to become comprehensible. A creep isn't a different kind of man – just one who has abandoned the difficult path of intimacy for the safer one of exploitation. We all hover at times on the brink of creephood. We must turn away from going down that road.

How we raise our kids

Prevention in the long term comes down to how we raise our kids. People who grow up in safety have self-worth and do not need to hurt others. Our first commitment as men must be to never act in a sexual way with children. Children must know, with total confidence, that they will not be mistreated and will not have their sexuality warped by domination and violence.

Secondly, it is best that as parents we give up smacking and hitting and find better ways of getting cooperation. Children who feel physically safe with their parents, who have not had their psychic boundaries kicked in by adult moods and invasions, are vastly more resistant to abuse, and certainly more likely to tell if it happens.

The third step is providing young people – the high-risk group for both abuse and becoming abusers – with a sense of belonging. This comes from the involvement of other adults who care and actively teach us. Young men in particular are often made to feel outsiders in society – and so they act like outlaws. Right now we give young men so little attention. Unless the young man looks like becoming a sports star, no older man is interested in him. Boys who succumb excessively to peer-group pressure invariably have weak or absent fathers, and no uncles or father-figures to take up the slack. Perhaps boys who participate in gang rapes should have their fathers go to jail along with them. A recent crime conference was told that young people should not live away from adults until they are in their mid-twenties. Before that point, they simply do not have the inner structure to handle independent living.

Boys drift into gangs because they instinctively seek leadership. The gang leader – a year older or a few centimetres taller – is not equipped to lead them in good directions. (Ghetto boys also join gangs for sheer self-defence because to fail to do so would be suicidal. The gang is their only protection, since the adults have long since lost control.) The gang exerts a price – it takes away your individuality. In the gang world, there is intense conformity based on fear. If you are different, you are not a man and will be persecuted, reviled, beaten up, even killed. (Yet among real men, difference is celebrated.) In such gangs, talk about girls has to be tough, exploitive. If you have no sexual experience, you fabricate some! To show involvement or tenderness to a girl indicates weakness.

Being secure in your sexual identity

Support and help from those of your own gender is essential to making you secure in your sexual identity (the chapter on initiation, 'The Wild Spirit of Man', pursues this further). Sex is an inward, personal thing as well as a meeting of man and woman. For a young man to relate to a young woman successfully, he must first be comfortable with

himself as a man. Yet this is rarely so. To be successful as
a lover, one must first see oneself as lovable, able to receive
and give tenderness, as the possessor of a 'magical soul
and a powerful heart'.

Bly stresses the need for young men to know that 'sexual
energy is good, that animal heat, fierceness and passionate
spontaneity is good'. With this confidence, there is less
aggression or competitiveness – no need to put women
down. When you can accept your extravagant, fierce yearnings then you can be unashamed and free of the need to
dominate. If your desired woman wants you, then that's
great. If she doesn't, then that's okay. Certainly someone
else will.

When a man has his inner esteem sorted out – with quiet
confidence instead of arrogance – then he can approach an
adult woman as an equal, without the need for power or
control. He is neither over-shy nor over-aggressive. He can
enter the dance of love with pride.

Owning your sexual charge

The so-called Playboy philosophy, for example, focuses on
the enticing Playmate. The good news of the Playboy gospel
is that the woman confers masculinity on the reader by sexually arousing him with her 'come-on' posture. In reality,
however, the reader has simply yielded his manly initiative
to the woman ... He has given his masculine spirit over to
the goddess and, thus, lost it.

Gordon Dalbey

There remains one last monster to wrestle. This one has
always been with us but, in our society, with its constant
media bombardment, it has grown into a large and many-
clawed beast!

Women hold such visual and tactile magic for men that
it is easy to make the serious mistake of handing one's
power over to them. They become the golden woman, the

goddess. From Marilyn Monroe to Madonna, our psyche seems to need this mythical figure.

In seeing women as the holders of sexual attraction – as having power over men's desire – men actually *give away* their own sexual energy. We put women on a pedestal and then resent them for being there. We have to become aware that sexual attraction lies not in the way a woman looks, but *in the way we choose to look at a woman*. A man's life goes a whole lot better when he realises that *he* is turning himself on and that he is a mind with a penis, not the other way around!

> No one arouses us. We arouse ourselves, no matter how convincingly we project such a capacity onto another. Men are not bewitched by women, but are bewitched by their own hoping-to-be engorged appetites, or more precisely, by their unwitting animation of and submission to such appetites, particularly those that promise some pleasurable numbing.
>
> Robert Masters, 'Ditching the Bewitching Myth'
> in *To Be a Man*

> Men say their penises have minds of their own, but men are geniuses at avoiding responsibility.
>
> Richard Rhodes

This misconception usually begins in adolescence. The culture of the soft-porn magazine provides a kind of schizophrenic split between the compliant, provocative perfection of the glossy image and the awkward, human, not-so-simple business of relating to real girls. As one writer in *XY Magazine* put it so plaintively, 'The pictures never loved me back'. The girlie-magazine ethos tells a young man, 'this is all you really want' – and yet delivers no warmth, no faithfulness, just a wisp of pleasure and then a long emptiness.

The young man who jumped to his death from a building in Adelaide, after disrupting an Elle MacPherson lingerie parade, had called out, 'You whore!', from the audience, before being ejected by security guards. His face, captured by a press photographer as he sprang from the crowd, was a blaze of pure fury. He was described in the press as having mental problems, but this does not mean that his feelings were invalid. Perhaps, like many disturbed young people, he just saw through the sham. In a sense, he was an early martyr of Men's Liberation.

We can expect far more men uniting with women to act against sexist advertising in the near future as well as tobacco companies and others who harm and exploit our children – may their spray cans never run dry!

Facing down the stallion

Minister and counsellor Gordon Dalbey, in his book *Healing the Masculine Soul*, tells a striking tale about freeing oneself from sexual manipulation. A young married man comes to him for advice because a woman at work has been seeking him out with tales of her husband's cruelty. They are spending more and more time together and she is becoming increasingly seductive (or he is becoming attracted to her – depending where you locate the responsibility!).

Dalbey explores the man's childhood and finds a pattern common to men in this situation. The man's father was considerably older than his mother, and was a remote type of man, who died while the young man was still in his early teens. The boy had always been his mother's comforter and confidant, more so after his father's death. So by the time he entered adulthood, he had already learned that comforting women – with subtle, sexual overtones – was his role in life. In a nutshell, his father's abandonment and his mother's psychic incest had set him up for just such a role.

Dalbey continued to counsel the man over several sessions. Fortunately (for the story), the man owned horses, and one morning an incident occurred which had direct bearing on his situation. A stallion, which had broken through a fence from his neighbour's property, was about to start mating with his mares. He found himself face to face with the highly excited, large black horse, armed only with a fence picket. He held his ground and herded the stallion back. Then (surprise, surprise!) he discovered that he could also face down the young woman who was coming (on) to him at work. She was furious and hurt, but in the end she sought help from a woman counsellor instead. She later thanked him for not playing a game which would have harmed them both.

The psychic incest that can occur between mothers and sons is a much under-explored area of damage to young men's development, setting them up for a lifetime of confusion if not understood. The melodramas which some men create for themselves with affairs, conquests or just plain marital tensions, often arise from equating self-worth with sexual 'success'. It certainly deflates the glamour when one realises that they are still trying to 'merge with Mama'!

There will always be flirtation, temptation and the potential for misuse of sex. The really mature men are those who know *they* are in charge of their own sexuality. They have 'corralled the stallion', to use Dalbey's phrase. Not castrated, just corralled – so you can take it where *you* want it to go. Men who have learned this bring a kind of inner calmness to their encounters with women which, far from being dulling, is erotic and tantalising to women in itself. Women are looking for this very capacity in a man. Someone who is capable of steady, fervent pursuit – not an oversized baby wanting to hang from their breast! Mills and Boon writers earn millions by acknowledging this facet of the feminine psyche – the irresistibility of a man who is willing to rein back his energy for the right time and place.

But that's enough horsing around!

In a nutshell

1 Don't mistake ejaculation for orgasm. Begin to explore increasing your relaxedness and awareness before, during and after lovemaking. Consider the possibility that there is vastly greater pleasure available, not from what happens on the outside but from what is allowed by you on the inside.

2 Sex isn't a separate part of you. Your heart, spirit, mind and body need to be along for the ride. Sex is a spiritual practice, capable of transforming your whole outlook and refreshing your sense of glory in being alive.

3 Deep sexual pleasure of the kind described above only occurs in a relationship with great emotional trust. This may take years to attain. It's worth the effort.

4 Masturbation is an essential and healthy part of men's sexuality throughout life. It is the way we develop appreciation of ourselves and our sensory potential, and realise that we own our own sexual energy.

5 Exploitive pornography (as opposed to respectful erotica), prostitution, much advertising, rock videos and the like degrade men just as much as women. They imply that cheap thrills are all we want and all women offer. Don't be fooled.

6 You have to guard against 'creepification' – the temptation to choose power over women, rather than the risky and vulnerable path of meeting them as

equals. Once you are proud of your gender and your sexuality you will not be afraid to risk rejection, and won't need to force or coerce women into sex. Neither will you abuse children.

7 Women don't turn you on. You turn yourself on, by the way you focus on women. Knowing this means you have a choice and a responsibility. To put it crudely but accurately – don't be led around by the dick.

Other voices

- Part of me lived outside my body – outside of emotion and feeling, cynical and hard, believing nothing, trusting nothing and no one ... Somewhere along the way ... the split healed, at least in lovemaking. It felt as if a dense, muffling integument had been peeled away.

  Instead of a compacted sensation localised in my groin, my ears roared, my skin flushed, my eyes dimmed, my innards loosened and flowed, and I was one instead of two. I felt boluses of semen moving up through the root and shaft of my penis like Roman-candle charges and then my entire body exploded and I wasn't two or one, I was none and everything. I was there and everywhere at once.

  Richard Rhodes

- [The men she had known] ... waited until dark, they drank to get their courage up, they laid on some perfunctory foreplay, and then they fucked, and whatever happened for the woman happened within that narrow range. I've got mine, now you get yours. They didn't even work to enlarge their own pleasure; once sheathed they drove more or less straight to ejaculation. I'm not surprised they had trouble getting it up and keeping it there.

  It's appalling that men willing to invest thought and energy in learning a sport ... won't invest thought and energy in learning how to play generously at sex. On the evidence, far too many men are sexually selfish and self-centred, reverting in the intimacy of the bedroom to mommy's darlings, taking rather than giving, not required, as girls are required from early childhood, to pay attention to needs other than their own.

  Richard Rhodes

• If one appreciates the harmonies of strings, sunlight on a leaf, the grace of the wind, the folds of a curtain, then one can enter the garden of love at unexpected moments. Moreover, after a man or woman has fallen in love, the leaf looks better, turns of phrase have more grace, shoulders are more beautiful. I noticed that we even love small towns. When we are in love, we love the grass, and the barns, and the lightpoles, and the small main streets abandoned all night.

Robert Bly

• My mouth on her body, my tongue savouring her crevices, was like plunging my face into a bowl of ripe summer fruits and inhaling their mingled fragrances – peaches, apples, pears. All of her was fresh. All of her was beautiful.

Richard Rhodes

• The erection, which the feminist and the macho alike have seen as such a one-note, one-purpose organ, is less a sword than a wand.

Michael Ventura in *Shadowdancing*

PST – the Masculine Curse!
Professor Walker Feinlein, from the University of Hobart, is known worldwide for his work on Pre-sexual tension, or PST. This widespread problem amongst males causes enormous mental instability, and is one of the reasons men must be excluded from most important decision-making and positions of responsibility. A man suffering from PST is likely to have wide mood-swings, be distractable and 'only want one thing'.

In his forthcoming book on the role of PST in history – entitled *Stop the World, I Want to Get off* – Feinlein has analysed PST's effect on famous events. Famous PST-sufferer Napoleon, on the eve of Waterloo (often mistranslated) actually said, 'Not tonight? – Josephine!!!!'

The Cuban missile crisis was another typical PST-driven incident. New documents from the Kremlin reveal that Kruschev was suffering serious PST at the time of the crisis, after abstaining from sex for over two months. Kennedy was likewise afflicted, not having seen action for over two hours!

Reported in *Heavy Metal*, the journal of the Risdon Zincworks

• What does it mean if a man falls in love with a radiant face across the room? It may mean he has some soul work to do. His soul is the issue. Instead of pursuing the woman and trying to get her alone, away from her husband, he needs to go alone himself perhaps to a mountain cabin, for three months, write poetry, canoe down a river and dream. That would save some women a lot of trouble. I am not saying that romantic love is always to be treated with suspicion and discounted. The whole matter is delicate.

Robert Bly

6
Men and Women

There are three things men need to understand if they are to get it right with women:
1 'standing up to' your wife or partner as an equal without intimidating her or being intimidated by her;
2 knowing the essential differences in male and female sexuality and so mastering 'the art of the chase'; and
3 realising she is not your mother and so making it through 'the long dark night'.

Intrigued? Well, here we go.

Man as a lovable dope

Most modern men, when faced with their wife's anger, complaints or general unhappiness, simply submit, mumble an apology and tiptoe away.* If they grumble, they do so into their beards. For the most part they act conciliatory and apologise for being such dopes. 'I'm sorry, dear!'

In the media, this has become a universal male stereotype for many decades – from the classic Dagwood cartoons to the 'Bill Cosby Show'. (Women's talk-show host Ray Martin played this role, masking the intelligence his job obviously required, with a little duck of the head and a sweet smile.)

---

* There is a small, remnant group of men who handle their differences with women through violence and intimidation. We will discuss the needs of this group later.

Everywhere you look around, the 'husband-as-a-lovable-dope' is an agreed-on type.

Real life, however, doesn't work like the sitcoms. The millions of men who adopt this stance find that it rarely, if ever, leads to happiness. Women with dopey husbands are not happy – they actually become *more* dissatisfied, more complaining. Often without even realising why, the hen-pecking behaviour escalates – for a simple reason. Deep down, women want to be *met* by someone strong. They want to be debated with, not just agreed with. They hunger for men who can take the initiative sometimes, make some decisions, tell them when they are not making sense. It's no fun being the only adult in the house. How can a woman relax or feel safe, when the man she is teamed with is so soft and weak?

I've counselled many strong, capable feminist women, who tell me that they have finally found the sensitive, caring, new-age man they *thought* they wanted and they are *bored stiff*! They are starting to drive slowly past building sites, wondering whether to whistle!

Men are actively aware of their failures in the relationship stakes. Whenever a group of men in their thirties and forties gather, it soon emerges how many have been badly wounded. Whether they show their sadness openly, or put on a belligerent front, it's the same thing. They know they are failing to satisfy the woman in their life, have failed to keep their relationships together and don't know what they have done wrong. Bly describes this phenomenon in men's groups.

> When the younger men spoke it was not uncommon for
> them to be weeping within five minutes ... grief flowed
> from their trouble in their marriages or relationships. They
> had learned to be receptive, but receptivity wasn't enough
> to carry their marriages through troubled times. In every
> relationship, something *fierce* is needed once in a while:
> both the man and the woman need to have it. But at the

point when it was needed, often the young man came up short. He was nurturing, but something else was required – for his relationship, and for his life.

The 'soft' male was able to say, 'I can feel your pain, and I consider your life as important as mine, and I will take care of you and comfort you'. But he could not say **what he wanted**, and stick by it. **Resolve** of that kind was a different matter.

How to stand up to your wife

Though it may surprise many male readers to know it, women are only human. This means they are sometimes dead right and sometimes completely wrong. Most men are caught up thinking women are either devils or saints and miss this simple point. Women are normal, fallible human beings. So it follows that being married to one you also have to keep your head on straight. You cannot just drift along and let them decide everything, which some men do. Marriage is not an excuse to stop thinking.

Not only can your wife be wrong, or immature, perverse, prejudiced, competitive or bloody-minded (just like you) – sometimes you and she just will see things differently because you **are** different. What is right for her may often be wrong for you – it's as simple as that. Women **often** don't understand men. How can they unless we explain ourselves to them? That doesn't mean you can't get along, just that you have to keep negotiating! Being falsely agreeable doesn't help either of you. Prepare for many long, patient debates!

I have heard literally hundreds of women say in frustration, 'My husband won't fight with me, he won't even argue. He just walks away.' Perhaps the husband walks away because he doesn't want to get physical like his father used to do. But avoidance does not solve this problem. Perhaps he had a nagging, carping mother and a weak father. Retreating is all he knows how to do. To have a happy marriage, a man has to be able to state his point of view, to debate, to leave aside hysteria and push on with an argument until something is resolved.

Gordon Dalbey tells of a woman who phones him after he has counselled her husband. 'It's obvious Sam's getting stronger, speaking up for himself and letting me know how he feels,' she said, hesitating. 'I know I've always wanted him to be that way ... but ... I guess there's a part of me that kind of enjoyed having the upper hand and being able to manipulate him into doing what I wanted. I want to be strong enough myself so that I don't do that any more.'

It's a measure of Dalbey's skill as a therapist that this woman is wanting to give up her power in order to experience a really equal relationship, based on intimacy and negotiation, not on emotional dominance.

The Warrior

There is an inner part of a healthy man or woman called the Warrior. The Warrior does not harm others. It does not need to. The Warrior 'guards the walls' of your emotional castle and protects you from mistreatment or abuse. The Warrior is not strong in children, which is why they need our protection.

Whenever I work with sexually abused clients, a final step in the healing is to help them become so angry and experience such burning rage that they mobilise all their physical and mental energy. They have never breathed so deeply, yelled so loud, focussed so clearly. Once this energy has started to flow, I have no fears that they will ever be abused again. People who have access to their inner rage are awe-inspiring. When the Warrior is mobilised, then the child within can finally feel safe. A woman who does this work can now begin to be close to and, if she wishes, marry a man. She will feel able and willing to bear a child. I have known fertility problems to disappear through this work –

as if a woman's body would not bear a child until her mind knew it could and would protect that child.

For a marriage to thrive, both partners need to bring their Warriors along. It's not that the other person wishes them harm, just that people getting close will inevitably overstep the other's boundaries and need to be reminded. Often its enough to say, 'Hey, you are crowding me', 'Don't make my mind up for me' or 'Let me choose my own clothes.'

> When my King is weak, I ask my wife or children what is the right thing to do. I've had strange adventures in buying sweaters.
>
> Robert Bly

Both partners can learn more respect for the other's need for selfhood. At times, there will be a real clash of realities, and more exploration will be needed. This is why couples need to fight in order to root out fixed attitudes or longer term misunderstandings, and pull them into the light of day. A good marriage *is* therapy, every living day.

We made a mistake in our Fifties' culture when we pursued the harmonious, sweet and loving ideal of marriage. The passionate, heated European-style marriage has more going for it. Jung said, 'American marriages are the saddest in the whole world, because the man does all his fighting at the office'.

Bly agrees:

> Conscious fighting is a great help in relationships between men and women. ... When a man and a woman are standing toe-to-toe arguing, what is it that the man wants? Often he does not know. He wants the conflict to end because he is afraid, because he doesn't know how to fight, because he 'doesn't believe in fighting', because he never saw his mother and father fight in a fruitful way, because his boundaries are so poorly maintained that every sword thrust penetrates to the very center of his chest ...'

The adult warrior inside both men and women, when

trained, can receive a (verbal) blow without sulking or col-
lapsing, knows how to fight for limited goals, keeps the
rules of combat in mind, and in general is able to keep the
fighting clean and to establish limits.

Passion needs rules

It's paradoxical that we can only let our feelings flow freely,
and only be truly passionate, when we have certain boundaries laid down. Trust has to be there. By limits, we mean:

- never being physical or threatening;
- never walking out mid-fight;
- not using put-down language;
- staying on the point and not bringing in other material;
- listening to the other's point of view while honouring
  your own; and
- taking time out, by agreement, if it becomes too heated
  – to think it over and returning to continue the argument.

These rules allow you to debate cleanly and respectfully,
until understanding is reached.

Fighting in marriage

Fighting in marriage can be a source of great learning and
growth. Marie-Louise von Franz tells a story about a friend
who had a series of marriages which were extremely tur-
bulent and painful. They always started well but each time
the arguing eventually lead to physical fighting and divorce.

The friend's fourth husband was different. The very first
time on which the wife 'threw a fit' (her words) and began
to be wildly abusive, the man simply walked quietly to his
room and began packing his things. He refused to fight
'dirty' as was being expected. His words are beautiful:

> I know I am supposed to act like a man now and shout and
> hit you, but I am not that sort of man. *I will not allow
> anyone to talk to me in the way you have*, and I am leaving.

The woman was so shocked she apologised. They are still together.

It's important to point out that if the woman in this story had been making a point, asking for a change, then the man needed to stay put and listen. But this was quite different. She was 'having a fit'. In Bly's words:

> Men and women both have this capacity for blind rage which achieves nothing. Arising out of centuries of two-way, inter-gender abuse, there is an archetypal core of rage in us which, if we take it into our relationships, destroys all love and feeling.

'I've had it with men', says she! 'Women!', he cries, 'Can't live with 'em, can't live without 'em!' It's the frustration of needing each other so much, but coming from a tradition of estrangement and misunderstanding that goes way back into our Judaeo-Christian roots. Germaine Greer said, 'All men hate all women some of the time'. And, we should add, vice versa. There is a long history of male-bashing by women, and female-bashing by men. But this isn't a personal thing and shouldn't be brought into personal affairs. The inner child in our partner cannot bear to face this much hate and he or she doesn't deserve it.

So there are two imperatives here. We **must** fight, debate and be true to ourselves, otherwise our closeness is just an act. But in fighting, we must show great restraint and always have respect. (My partner, Shaaron, and I wrote a book about this, called *The Making of Love*, which has rules for fighting and many stories by way of illustration.)

Sam Keen puts it well. 'Romance is all "yes" and heavy breathing – an affair built around the illusion of unbroken affirmation. Marriage is "yes" and "no" and "maybe" – a relationship of trust that is steeped in the primal ambivalence of love and hate.'

'Love and hate' doesn't have to be all that dramatic. It's as simple as the switching between 'I just want to lie with you here forever' and 'Will you, for Chrissake, leave my desk as it is – I know where to find things!'

'But I was just tidying it up.'

'Well, *don't*!'

We all want to be close, but no-one likes the feeling of being swamped.

Stopping male violence

An important consideration enters here into our discussion of men and women solving their differences. When men feel intimidated, they will often have the physical and temperamental potential to swing the other way – and counter-attack – with violence. Domestic violence – and its close relatives, financial control and emotional blackmail – are as Australian as going to the beach. We are only just learning how to deal with them.

Let us take you on a small excursion that may give you some cause for hope. It's a warm evening in Perth, Western Australia. A group of men are meeting at a health centre. In the room there are two leaders and eight men, all of whom are there because of a history of violence against wives and children. As we join them, one of the leaders is talking with a man in the group who looks awkward, his arms crossed tightly across his chest.

'So, Dave, you say you "roughed her up". What does "roughed her up" mean?'

'I pushed her around a bit, nothing bad.'

'How did you push her?'

'With my hand. She was swearing at me. She'd been late home from her class.'

'How hard did you push her?'

'Not very hard. She just fell back against the wall and she started to cry.'

'Did she look scared?'

'Yes.'

'So you pushed her hard enough to make her feel pretty scared of you.'

'Yes.'

'Do you think she felt good being scared of you like that?'

'No.'

'How do you feel that you made the woman you love so scared, just because you are bigger than she is and you used violence.'

'Not good.'

'Is that something you'd like to learn to handle better – that kind of situation?'

'Yes. That's why I'm here.'

'Okay.'

The Duluth model

The group described above studies intensively a diagram called 'A wheel of power and control' (see 'Relating with Respect'). Placed around the wheel are all the ways that – instead of relating on equal terms with their partners – they opt instead for power-tactics, of which violence is just one. It's acknowledged that women have their own power-tactics too. However, for the pattern to be broken, men must commit themselves to giving up violence as a method. Once this commitment is given, then huge efforts are made to build communication skills, assertiveness and the healing of the man's own abusive memories. (Almost always these men have witnessed or received abuse in their childhood families.)

The aim is to bring men and women to a point where they can relate with respect and without needing to use power or control over the other. Most women have wanted this to happen for a long time. The difference, when this is done from a Men's Movement perspective, is that it's done by men healing men and men confronting men.

This approach to work with violent men is done not as an alternative to the law, but as part of a wider legal and corrective system. Men in these programs know that if they offend, they will be charged and locked up. The difference here is that they are not just released to offend again, as in most parts of the world, but will be actively and con-frontingly rehabilitated.

> If the power struggle with his woman has not been satisfac-torily enough resolved, and if he has not been able to formulate and to adequately defend his boundaries, the dis-empowered man's goodwill toward his mate may, at this point, completely evaporate. In a vain effort to feel his legitimate power, he may try to use the energy generated by his growing rage illegitimately through acts of verbal and/or physical abuse. Alternatively, he may play dead, with-drawing from the field of battle and exhibiting symptoms of major depression. Usually his behaviour will oscillate be-tween these two extremes.
>
> Douglas Gillette in *Wingspan*

It's amazing to realise the underlying issues from which domestic violence arises. Often they are infantile 'baby' issues: 'She didn't fix my meal right'. 'She wants to go out with her friends and leave me all alone at home.' 'She talked to another guy.' 'She wants to visit her mother.'

It is truly pathetic and sad to realise how threatened these men feel in their marriages and their lives as a whole. Many men in such groups state that they have never had friends who could listen to their situations before coming to the program. The men they meet in the groups are, paradoxi-cally, more confronting and more supportive than any they have met. With this kind of male friendship, they are less dependent and burdensome to their wives. This is close to the heart of what Men's Liberation is all about.

Men changing men

Defeating violence is a central part of the Men's Movement. Clear ethics are emerging from the swamp of self-justifica-

tion that has been around for so long. Men are saying
clearly now to their brothers – 'It's wrong to hit women.
It's wrong to hit or be sexual with children. We are your
friends and that is why we tell you this. And if need be
we will stop you, with legal means, if you refuse to stop
yourself.'

Such honesty is a 180-degree turn from the phony friendship of the bar or the sports club. Men's Movement ethics
will make a powerful difference. For instance, no-one who
counts himself part of the Movement would sleep with
another man's wife. If a 'foxy' young woman sashays up
to you at a bar – and tells you how her husband is no
good or doesn't understand her – then you tell her she
needs to go and talk it through with him. It won't help to
tell *you* about it!

Which brings us around to sex.

Sex and the chase

A story ...

With my wife I am giving a weekend workshop for
married couples from a church congregation. They are all
nice people. In fact, a bit too nice – especially the men.
Good-hearted but just too agreeable. The soft slippers, neat
garden, never-a-cross-word type of guy.

We are working through a list of topics and it's the
Sunday afternoon, getting late. One of the topics on the list
is 'Sexuality and the Chase'. We haven't got to this topic
yet. A man in his late thirties, sitting in a beanbag leaning
comfortably against his sparky young wife, asks, 'When are
we going to do sexuality?'

'Oh,' I say, with a grin, 'we might get round to it in a
little while!' (I'm teasing him, but I don't know why.) 'It
depends if there's enough time.'

'Oh, okay,' he says, and slumps back in his beanbag. My
sense of mischief grows.

'Is this what he does in bed?', I ask his wife, grinning.

'*Yes, it is*!', she says.

She seems to know what I mean. He looks bewildered , so I elaborate.

'Well, you wanted to do something about sex. I wasn't sure. So you quit. You gave up. Don't you know you're supposed to persist? You want it handed to you on a plate?' He starts to blush, but he's not unhappy. He's catching on fast.

'You see, that's how sex works,' I go on (smug in my expert role!). 'You need to be considerate and patient, sure, but you don't give up. You have a part of you that is wild and free and just wants to go for it!' (I want to use words like 'wild fucking' but it's a church group!)

'The thing you don't realise is that, treated properly, at the right time, that is what she wants too.' (I have to stop speaking at that point, because his wife, out of his range of view just beside him, is biting her lip and nodding *Yes*!)

One intense sexual storm in a hay-barn means more to her than three years of tepid lovemaking. She wants passion and purpose in a man, and she carries a weighty desire in her, a passion somewhere between erotic feeling and religious intensity.

Robert Bly

Persist

The knack of being a lover, a suitor (which is the role of every husband for always, not just in courtship), is to persist, without being a pest. Even if it takes weeks. Biology made women slow to burn and men quick to explode. A skilful lover needs to damp down his fire but not let it go out. Foreplay and pursuit take place over days. Even when lovemaking has started in earnest, he holds back. Gradually, as tenderness, skill and intensity of touch set her alight, he can abandon himself more and more to his passion, catching up with her in joyous abandon.

One of the best love scenes on film is in *Coming Home* with Jane Fonda and Jon Voigt. Voigt plays a paraplegic Vietnam veteran who has no feeling below the waist. But he is no less a lover. (It's a lesson in awakening. You, dear reader, presumably still have your legs, so you've no excuses.)

Sleeping Beauty

It's all right there in the fairytale, *Sleeping Beauty*. If you're the man, you have to hack through those thorns, sweat and bleed until you get to the princess in the castle. (Feminist academics thought this fairytale was bad news with a capital B. They didn't much like the apparent passivity of the woman. This is a complete mythunderstanding. There is nothing passive about this lady. She is so powerful that the whiff of a rumour of the legend of her beauty makes this man work for weeks! At a deep level, she calls the shots. At another level, he is coming with his magic wand to transform them both. They are equal but they have different kinds of power.)

The princess hasn't even been really asleep for all that time. She was off getting her degree, talking to her friends, playing tennis. She just rushes back at the last minute and pretends to be asleep! On another level, though, she was waiting to be awakened (and he was too). In he comes and looks at her lying there. Then he bends to kiss her – if he dares. Some men see beauty and just get so scared they slip back through the thorns to the safer company of their horse! (Many beautiful women are ignored by good men who are too afraid. They have to put up with predators instead.) But if he doesn't chicken out and if he kisses her, she will awaken. And when she awakens you better be ready. This woman has been waiting for a hundred years and boy is she **hungry**!

His mother, as the maternal form of the feminine, he has of course experienced, but that is all. And now he is about to

meet the feminine in a non-maternal form – in its powerful,
blossoming, savvy, wild, instigating, erotic, playful form.
She is the savvy woman on the earth plane.

Robert Bly in Iron John

Confidence

Lovemaking and courtship take more than a little confidence
on the man's part. As Marvin Allen said, 'Between first
meeting a gal and getting where you want to be, there are
573 chances of rejection!' If you've come through some
kind of initiation, if you hold your own sexuality as sacred
and are proud of your own gender, then you come to the
woman with fascination and with respect – but on equal
terms. You respect and desire her but you respect yourself
too. It takes the desperation out of it.

Protectiveness

Protectiveness helps too. Many women I have talked to are
delighted by the male character in the film, *The Bodyguard*,
played by Kevin Costner. He is intensely nurturing, protective
and hard-headed. It's the soft/strong combination again.
And, according to my informants, a winning combination.

A space of your own

If a human being takes action, the soul takes action. Ritual
space gives something back to the man or woman who, prepared by discipline and quiet, enters it.

Robert Bly

It's important for anyone's sense of self that they have a
space to be in that is their own. Many men have no space
of their own in the house – clearly from the decor and
furnishings, the bedroom is usually the woman's space.
(The shed is a good start, but is still more of a retreat, not

really part of the house.) Along with having a room of one's own, goes time of one's own. Setting aside time each day to be yourself and do your thinking means you have a more equal footing in the household and less need to retreat to the office or the pub.

> There is a need for a *'place'*. Men feel a loss of home. The male spirit or soul doesn't feel that it has a home. The man goes to work and deals with that set of responsibilities and difficulties. Then he goes home, and deals with that set of responsibilities and difficulties. He doesn't have a sense of home – as in a dwelling place – where he gets to dwell within himself.
>
> Robert Bly

I negotiated for myself a room of my own. A bedroom, office, store for my things. Walls for my quotations, pictures, statues, tools. My music. Interesting that a teenager has this, but a man doesn't. A shared bedroom tends to meet the woman's sensibilities – she is often the only one who has sensibilities.

Men *and* women need a place of their own in a house. Where they can invite the other, but also feel private and be restored by their sense of being themselves, in their own space.

In conclusion, there will always be some tension in male–female relationships – adult love isn't meant to have the same sugary-sweet harmony of a mother and baby. When an adult man and woman meet, two powerful magicians are in the room, but they need each other to release their full magic.

The core message of feminism is true. We *are* equal. We can reverse roles if we want to, for as long as feels good. Everything we have said in the above passages can be reversed. He can be asleep in the castle and she might, some time, come and wake him up. Don't let your archetypes be stereotypes! But don't be afraid to be a man either – to tap the energy and spark of being your own gender and work the ancient dynamic of male and female to the maximum benefit of all.

Getting through the 'long dark night'

Most contemporary men get together with a woman first and then grow up second – if we're lucky and she is patient! So it's realistic that some crises of growth will occur, which we will have to find our way through within the relationship. There is one outstandingly common crisis, which is probably the reason behind ninety percent of marriage breakups (however much other reasons are cited). I call this stage 'the long dark night'. It would be more edifying if it were the 'long dark night of the soul', but, the fact is, it's really just the long dark night of the penis! Let me explain.

We fall in love mostly by good luck. It just happens. So maintaining love is often left to luck too. Unlike those cultures where marriages are arranged, we don't realise that love is a craft which takes practice. Eventually, then, most men and women lose the spark – they fall out of love.

The man usually denies this to himself and is happy enough as long as his partner stays sexually available. It may be that, for men, sex has a kind of sedating, reward-at-the-end-of-the-day quality (as expressed in the hugely popular song, 'My Baby Takes the Morning Train' by Sheena Easton). Sex is a compensation for the treadmill quality of the rest of life – with a mortgage, young children and long-service just fifteen years away!

Very often though, today's woman tires of routine sex. The very thing that makes him a good husband – his devotion to being a stable provider – wears out his spirit and makes him boring. Finding little reward in their boring lives or their sex-life, she starts to cool down. She exerts her perfect right to not make love. The man sulks, suffers, grouches and schemes, to no avail.

There are two ways to react to this situation. For a man with inner resources, this is a temporary setback. He admits in the first place that sex **was** actually routine, that the relationship had gone hollow – and perhaps he was not as content as he had been telling himself. He begins the concerted work to get things restarted: planning holidays or weekends together; relieving her of the pressures of children; cutting back his work commitments so as to be more energetic and interesting at home; and stopping being such a slob. Even larger changes of lifestyle are possible. There are plenty of avenues.

For many men though, lacking inner security, the loss of sexual contact is devastating – far beyond its actual meaning. The average man – shut down to his feelings since childhood, numb and hard in his body – **only really feels alive when he is having sex**. Sex is the only opening to his inner body. Now this avenue is lost too!

The problem may go deeper still. Lacking adequate fathering, he has never really unbonded from his mother. He has simply transferred his mother-needs onto his wife. So as well as a loss of **sex**, he experiences a loss of **love** at an infantile level. It's as if he's been left in his crib to starve. Many men in their late thirties and early forties have encountered this despair. The drowned school teacher at the start of this book may be an instance of this. The depression that arises is so complete, all previous enjoyments and reasons for living seem to have turned to ashes.

The man in this position usually acts in a weak and helpless way. This just makes him even less appealing to his wife, however much she may sympathise. (She would do him no favour by relenting.) Or he may get nasty, become violent, hide money or, often as not, begin an affair. This is almost always a serious mistake. With the new woman, he will very likely simply replay the pattern. Five years down the track, he will be at the same place. He finds himself at forty-five, walking the boards with another sleepless baby, thinking, 'I've been here before!'

We may be unduly pessimistic here. The point is important though: it isn't a woman you need at this time in your life – for the following reasons.

This whole catastrophe of the 'long dark night of the penis' is the result of a totally mistaken belief on the part of the man – *that you can't live without a woman's love*. The remedy, vitally important – since we are talking about 40 000 divorces a year here – is for other men to step in and give emotional support.

This is not the same as getting you drunk. Good friends at these times will listen to you talk about your problems but also have fun, take you 'up the bush', eat, cook and play. They will also – when the time is right – point out that it's time you got back to your family and sorted things out. It's as if male friends and elders bathe your wounds, refresh you, give you a hug and then throw you back into the ring!

Choose your friends carefully. Some friends are on the side of your marriage and your happiness. However, a whole other group – both married and single – are losers with women and are *glad* to see you having problems too. They don't *want* you to stay married. Misogynous men can be found in any bar in Australia. Avoid them.

The man who has made it through

For the man who makes it through the 'long dark night' , the rewards are great. He loses the babylike quality that many men have. He is no longer in any hurry. Around women, he is especially different. He is no longer 'mother-bound' or soggy, although he remains playful and ironic. Comfortable in his aloneness, he approaches women as equals. Since he offers a woman real companionship and is less demanding, he is much more attractive. There's sweet irony here that when you can 'take it or leave it', when love and affection are no longer a matter of life and death, then it all comes to you!

In a nutshell

1 Don't agree with your wife for the sake of peace. Say what is true for you. You have to walk a line – not giving in out of weakness and not getting violent or intimidating. Both are signs of unnecessary fear.

2 Men are less skilled in verbal debate, being given less training as boys. Hang in there till you get the knack.

3 Decide now never to use violence against a woman or a child. If you have trouble with this, join a men's group which addresses this problem. We recommend groups run on what is called The Duluth Model. (See 'Relating with Respect'.)

4 In sex and loving, much of the time the man has to make the running. This is a matter of biology. Learn to be persistent and courtly. Be protective. Don't crowd her. Work to win her over. If sometimes you don't succeed, don't take it personally.

5 Most marriages go through phases of sexual distance or shutting down. Don't mistake this for not being lovable. At the same time, don't depress yourself and just tolerate an unhappy sex life. Work to find out what is wrong, and fix it.

6 Many men have their wife and mother mixed-up, and think they'll die without a breast to suckle on. If sexual advances are perceived by your partner as demanding and overly needy, it can be a real turn-off. This is a good time to do some growing up, realising your emotional independence from sex. Not *needing* sex actually makes you much more attractive.

Other voices

- For many men the fight with a female partner often follows four steps:
  First act – 'You're right, I had no right to do that.'
  Second act – 'I've always been like that.'
  Third act – 'My father made me like this, he was never there for me.'
  Fourth act – 'All men are shits.'

  (Adapted from Robert Bly)

- So if a man can't trust anyone with a cock to be caring, compassionate and considerate, he looks towards the other gender for this emotional support and for models of behaviour. The mother is more available, softer and will even listen to him sometimes. He turns to the feminine for comfort, nurturing, understanding and love, and makes his life circle around women, always watching and valuing their every word, gesture and movement, which he may imitate later, which then usually attracts other women (like his mother) to him.

  John Lee in *At My Father's Wedding*

- The masculine lover says, 'After decades of constant compromise of my essential self, I will not do so to be loved by you. I'll compromise on where we live, where we eat, how many children we have, what movie we see, where our children will go to school, but not on matters that jeopardise my soul – I need you to stop drinking in this house. I need the abuse to stop. I demand safety. I need to be nurtured. I need love. I need to express my anger. I need you to express yours. I need mutual respect and equality. I will not settle for less than what I know I deserve, which is health. I will not compromise my recovery to be in a relationship."

  John Lee in *At My Father's Wedding*

The Hazards of Being Male
(Herb Goldberg)
There is a commonly expressed notion that men will somehow
be freed as a by-product of the feminist movement. This is a
comforting fantasy for the male but I see no basis for it in reality. It simply disguises the fear of actively determining his own
change. Indeed by responding inertly and passively, the male
will be moved, but not in a meaningful and productive direction. If there is to be a constructive change for the male, he
will have to chart his own way, develop his own style, and experience his own anxieties, fear, and rage, because this time
mommy won't do it! The most remarkable and significant aspect
of the feminist movement to date has been woman's daring willingness to own up to her resistance and resentment toward her
time-honoured, sanctified roles of wife and even mother. The
male, however, has yet to fully realise, acknowledge, and rebel
against the distress, and stifling aspects of many of the roles
he plays – from good husband to good daddy. Because of the
inner pressure to constantly affirm his dominance, and masculinity, he continues to act as if he can stand up under, fulfil, and
even enjoy all the expectations placed on him, no matter how
contradictory and devitalising they are.

Indeed, something awful happens to many men after they
get married. As a sensitive and aware married woman I interviewed described the married men in her neighbourhood:
'They're all so passive. They have to hate their wives because
those guys are hardly even people. A typical weekend day for
them seems to mean trimming hedges, mowing the lawns and
puttering with their cars'.

Furthermore many married men seem to become progressively more childlike, dependent and helpless in their
interactions with their wives. Wives discussing their husbands
with me in private often make comments such as, 'He acts like
a baby', 'He's become so dependent on me it scares me. He
won't do anything for himself', 'He acts as if he's totally helpless', and 'He's always hanging around the house and getting
in the way. I wish he had some more friends'.

Many of these men ask their wives for permission whenever they want to do things on their own. When they describe the positive aspects of their marriage relationship it often sounds something like, 'She lets me do a lot of things on my own and doesn't stay on my back, like a lot of other wives that I know'. In essence, the wife has been given the role of permission-giver or mother-figure by the male.

Progressively, the married man begins to distrust his own judgement and taste. He starts to believe that he is an unaesthetic clod who is only good in the business or working world and that his taste does not measure up to hers. Like mother, she knows best. As one real-estate person expressed it to me, 'I never sell to the husband. I always sell to the wife. If he likes the house, it doesn't mean anything. But if she likes it, I've got a sale.'

Because he is caught in a relationship that may not be intrinsically satisfying to him, although he is not always in conscious touch with his anger, resentment and desire for autonomy, his negative feelings continually emerge indirectly in the form of passive aggression. He is 'in' the relationship but not 'of' it. The passive expression of his frustration and discontent assumes many forms:

1 Extreme moodiness and occasional outbursts of rage that are precipitated by relatively minor things such as a misplaced sock, laundry done late, a button that hasn't been sewn on, a toy left on the floor or a late meal.
2 Grabbing for the mail, a drink, and then hiding behind the newspaper or in front of a television set almost immediately after coming home from work.
3 Increasing expression of his wanting to be 'left alone' when he's at home.
4 Increasing complaints of fatigue and physical ailments such as backaches, stomach aches and headaches.
5 A drifting of attention when his wife is speaking to him causing him to ask her frequently to repeat herself, an indication that his mind is wandering and that he is not concentrating.

MEN AND WOMEN   **103**

6   Having to be reminded constantly about the same things which he continually seems to forget, such as hanging up his clothes, taking out the garbage, etc.

7   A general resistance to talking about his day when he comes home in the evening.

8   Avoidance of sexual intimacy manifested indirectly by either coming to bed after she's fallen asleep, or falling asleep before she's come to bed. Other manifestations include bringing home work from the office, and doing it into the night, and staying up late to read or watch television.

9   An avoidance of eye contact with his wife.

10   An increasing tendency to confine his social life with his wife to activities such as going out to eat or to a movie, which do not require active interaction between them.

11   Generalised feelings of boredom. The boredom often disguises an impulse or desire to do things or be places other than where he is. Since he is unable to own up to his real needs, he does nothing and sits home bored instead.

Unable to assert himself openly or to own up to his discomfort, his hidden resentment emerges in a myriad of underground ways. The message he is transmitting indirectly to his wife is 'I'm afraid to do what I really want to do, or express how I really feel, so I'll avoid feeling guilty by staying at home. But you aren't going to get any satisfaction from my presence either.'

• The man without an activated emotional body may alternate between abusive behaviour and impotent gentleness that isn't really gentle. Robert Moore remarked that two distinguishing marks of the uninitiated man are wife-beating and the contrary softness.

Robert Bly in *Wingspan*

• The first strong emotion I felt for G---- after desire, was respect. For her courage. For having survived with her capacity to love intact.

Richard Rhodes

7

Being a Real Father

What does fathering mean? Listen to the language we use every day and it will tell you a lot. If we talk of 'mothering' children, we get a picture of caring, nurturing and spending long hours in close, sensitive contact. The word 'fathering' means something quite different. You can 'father' a child in two minutes (in the back of a panel van)! At its most extreme, a father is just a sperm donor. Nothing more. (In fact many people today do not see any problem with single women – or lesbian couples – seeking donor insemination, leaving fathers out completely.) However, fathering is much more than this. It's an essential part of raising children of either sex. Yet the art of fathering has all but disappeared.

John Embling is a worker with kids in inner-city Melbourne. His books include *Tom – a child's life regained* and *Fragmented Lives*. John uses his own masculine nurturing ability to pull kids back from homelessness, violence and imprisonment. Here are his thoughts on fathers:

> I spend most of my life with children, young adults, mothers – but where are the fathers? I have known only four or

five fathers-as-parents, as providers, as role models, over those ten years.

I have seen so many young children who need men in their home lives, men who are capable of psychologically meeting their needs. A community of men alone is unltimately an unhealthy one for children, a community of women alone is similarly restricted.

Even the strongest, most capable single parent finds it difficult to give his or her child all that is needed to make a human being. I know divorced couples who have come to an equitable arrangement for the stable, intimate, everyday management and rearing of their children. But what about the single, deserted, penniless mother on the top floor of the Kensington Housing Commisson flats. Where do her children look for relationships with father figures?

I often look around for the fathers in the lives of our children. I feel a sense of profound loss, of defeat, of inhumanity, as I see men devoid of personal contact with their children. Their loss, the loss of something central to human process, is also our loss. Something is being crippled, and all the money, technology, bureaucracy, professionalism, ideology in the world won't make it right again.

John Embling in *Fragmented Lives*

The role of father has sunk to a very low point. Are fathers necessary? According to some feminists, 'A world without men, would be a world full of fat, happy women!' To which we'd add, '... and very screwed-up children'. In this chapter we argue that girls need fathers for very specific reasons in their development – reasons that cannot be fulfilled by mothers on their own. Even more importantly, we believe that boys who do not get very active fathering – either by their own father or someone who is willing to step in – will never get their lives as men to work. It's as simple and as absolute as that.

Let's assume you are a father or plan to be one. You have love and good intentions. But still you may be starting in a virtual vacuum. Many elements you wish to bring to parenting your children – consistency, firmness, warmth and involvement – you may have never received from a male figure yourself. You have the love but not the methods. No-one installed the software. There is a problem in turning your love into action.

Most of the men I meet in men's groups are fathers. The Men's Movement has made this a major focus, especially by fostering discussion about 'what works'. Fathers today are keen, even desperate, to 'get it right' because they feel so acutely that their own childhoods were inadequate and painful. Men's groups also have begun to help each other practically with their children ('uncling', if you like). Another benefit of men's groups is that they offer retreats, camping trips, etc., creating many opportunities for surrogate fathering *for each other*, for learning to care about and listen to each other, for speaking more honestly and 'cutting the bullshit', for being less competitive and more practically and emotionally helpful.

Dropping the old roles

Probably the first step we must take to get it together as a father is to shed some of the old role models. These were often limiting and impoverished, and yet sit heavily like old videotape collections in our head.

In his beautiful book, *At My Father's Wedding*, John Lee describes **four kinds of defective father** that predominated in years past. Here they are paraphrased:

The man who would be king

This was the man who, having (presumably) worked hard all day, returned home to be waited on by his loyal wife-servant and seen-but-not heard children. He was king of the house and ruled his castle kingdom from the Jason recliner. His family tip-toed around him, careful not to 'bother' him. The only time this father got really involved was to dish out punishments or pardons. This was also the 'wait until your father gets home' father.

> My dad had an over-developed attachment to his roof. He talked about his roof a lot, and referred to it constantly when I dared question the King's decree for me. 'This is my house. You live under my roof. As long as you are under my roof you'll do as you're told. When you get your own roof you can do whatever you want to, but while you're under my roof you'll do what I say when I say it.' 'Damn', I thought to myself. 'I can't wait to get my own roof.'

The critical father

Full of put-downs and nit-picking, driven by his own frustration and anger. This father was certainly active in the family, but in totally negative, frightening ways. 'Is that the best you can do?' 'Can't you get anything right?' 'You stupid idiot, look what you've done!' Whatever was frustrating him – his job, his own father, his lack of success in life, even just his hopes for his children – even the sweet wine of his love was turned into an acid which ate away at his family's wellbeing.

The passive father

This guy gave up all duties, responsibilities and power to his wife, the mother. Backing down also to the kids, his boss, relatives, society, the government and so on. This is Bart Simpson's dad. He lost his balls somewhere, way back, and now it's all just too hard to even think about. Apart from an occasional comment or bleating justification of himself, he was never really there. Unable to stand the heat, he would retreat into a newspaper, TV, alcohol or his garden shed. His kids grew up hating him for his lack of backbone.

The absent father

This man might have been a capable, even powerful man, but not in the family arena. He was off having a career, leaving early and returning late at night. When he made love to your mother to start you, he was thinking about something else! He wasn't at your sports events or your school concert. He might have paid for all kinds of goodies for you and even been quite polite and kindly if you chanced to meet him in the hallway one night! But he wasn't any use to you as a father because *a father has to be there*.

These days it seems almost too much to ask – a father who is active and involved, a father who is his own man and also is willing to be a partner to his wife and a father to his kids.

> The passive man may skip over parenting. Parenting means feeling, but it also means doing all sorts of boring tasks – taking children to school, buying them jackets, attending band concerts, dealing with curfew, setting rules of behaviour, deciding on responses when these rules are broken, checking on who a child's friends are, listening to the child's talk in an active way, etc. The passive man leaves his wife to do that.
>
> Robert Bly in *Wingspan*

We can only imagine what the world would be like if we had not only fathers, but ministers of religion, bosses at work, school principals, politicians and prime ministers whom we could actually believe in – who embodied kindness, backbone, irony, humour, wisdom, righteous anger and protectiveness. There might be some disagreement as to style. (Robert Bly's impact has come very largely through his personal manner. His fatherliness is striking. He has made a craft out of the role of storyteller – the wise, ironic old man, teasing and challenging young men, furious at the Vietnam generals for their betrayal, an ancient figure in eccentric clothes, spouting poetry, happily plump and old in an age that deifies youth.)

How men and boys were split

For hundreds of thousands of years the human race lived in small nomadic groups – two or three dozen to a group.

Perhaps in your whole life, if you had lived in those times, you would meet only two hundred people. Even when the New Stone Age ended and recorded history began, we still lived for four thousand years in villages and small towns. The great cities of ancient history – Athens, Crete and Rome – were small towns by our present standards.

In the highly stable lifestyle of the tribe and the village, fathers and sons lived and worked in close proximity. The fathers, uncles and grandfathers taught the young men their own work or trade and, at the same time, how to be a man. It was a long apprenticeship. Forty-year-olds were still learning. Old men and women led by virtue of their vast knowledge and experience. All day, every day, boys were surrounded by men, actively (and usually enjoyably) encouraging and teaching them. They drank in deeply the tone, style and manner of being a man, from a dozen available role models, who were tough and tender with them as needed. Surprisingly to most of us, it's now thought that life in hunter-gathering times was comfortable, even leisurely. For instance, most people could meet their food and shelter needs with only a couple of hours work per day. We've clearly gone backwards! The detailed knowledge and consummate skill of the people accumulated over aeons and systematically handed down, one-to-one, to each child, meant that life was abundant and pleasurable.

Not all was perfect. Ancient cultures had their problems too, but they had a balance and a life-preserving quality that had been honed over hundreds of generations. Then in an unprecedented way (in the ecological blink of an eye), it all began to change. The shift to agriculture, the birth of cities and then (a mere five generations ago) the Industrial Revolution arrived and changed everything forever. Villagers were evicted to free up the land for wool, which was more profitable than crops. Wool needed a fraction of the labour force to tend. The towns needed a workforce – factory workers, clerks, miners and labourers. It was a matter of change or starve. (The same pattern is still taking place today in Asia and elsewhere.)

Fathers for the first time in history worked away from their sons, waking before first light and returning after dark. Schooling was introduced – not so much for humanitarian reasons but because it was found to prepare children better to be placid factory workers when they were nine or ten years old.

For the first time in human history a generation of boys grew up without being fathered in the true sense. Today we take this arrangement for granted. Fathers work, mothers raise children (or put them in childcare for other women to raise). Female school teachers civilise our boys. Boys have a choice: to comply and be good little boys or else play up and misbehave. The 'misbehavers' form gangs for solace and self-protection, looking for the masculine energy they do not realise they are missing.

Father-absence today

From a son's point of view, little has changed for 150 years. Now fathers work in cleaner, safer environments – but the effect on the family is the same. It could even be worse. A man who takes up desk work in an office has little in common with his son and often cannot even explain to his son what he is doing. Daddy 'goes to work', where he simply disappears into incomprehensible activity, for nine or ten hours a day.

In the mid-1970s the Mattel toy company wanted to market a family of dolls called 'The Heart Family'. First they trialled the sets, which comprised (naturally!) a mother, father and two children. The test children, in numerous samples, took the father doll and set him aside. Then they played with the mother and children. When asked, 'What about the father doll?', they replied, 'He's at work', and left the doll untouched in a corner! Father's work had no substance or meaning, and he was rarely used in the make-believe play. (Eventually, of course, the problem was solved. The father dolls were sold separately with big muscles, armour and a gun!)

Bly says that 'If the father in a family inhabits the house for only an hour or two in the evenings, then women's values, marvellous as they are, will often become the only values active in the house'. What children get from a career father is not his happiness, nor his teaching, nor his substance, but only his *mood*. And at seven o'clock at night, that mood is mostly irritation and fatigue.

The girls learn to be a woman from Mum – but the boys cannot learn to be a man from Mum, however good a mum she is. Feminism took root and thrived through the networking of women who were already well versed in giving verbal support, in relating woman-to-woman at an intimate level. In a sense, it was easy for them to do this. Men have few skills in relating man-to-man, especially across age groups. Where would they ever get practice?

We have different degrees of father-absence in our society. With our high level of marriage breakdown, perhaps a third of all children grow up with a father absent or intermittent in family life. One study found that after one year following divorce, over thirty percent of fathers had *no further contact* with their children!

We've said earlier that teenage gangs are made up of boys whose fathers are either absent or have withdrawn emotionally. The gang members' behaviour (which they themselves do not consciously understand) is clearly designed to provoke older adult males into taking notice of them. This is a dynamic understood by all good country policemen.

Peer-group pressure, which affects all children, only has a *problematic* effect on those who have a poor relationship with their *same-sex parent*. A teenage boy who enjoys the company of his father and his father's friends does not need to look towards an eighteen-year-old gang leader for leadership.

The bad news is that even when things are going well in the family, it may not be enough. Even when a father is present, committed and available at weekends and evenings in a healthy marriage and with all the ideal conditions, sons still miss out. It's highly likely that boys have a biological need for *several hours* of one-to-one male contact *per day*. Put another way, to have a demanding job, commute to work in a city and raise sons well is an impossibility. Something has to give.

Confident maleness

It gets worse. A number of psychoanalysts and family therapists around the world have noted that father-absence creates some special side effects. It isn't just that the absent father is a neutral persona. You can't be neutral in a family. Occupants of the same household can only either love or hate each other. A son either loves or hates his father – it's never neutral. Having something you deeply need, so near and yet so far, produces a great intensity of feeling.

The modern career dad has these problems to contend with. Men show their love by working hard and long. And they do not get appreciated for it – since it is their presence, not their bounty that is hungered for by their children. Kids still ask for the computer game or the fancy joggers, but with enough father-time they soon forget these substitutes. Women need to be very clear about what they ask of their husbands – since the men are likely, by default, to assume that it is their earning capacity that is their biggest contribution.

A friend of ours married a woman who once mentioned during the courtship that she would never have married a poor man. He became a compulsive gambler to keep up the impression of success. This lead to embezzling and a prison sentence. It was a tough lesson.

The Fifties' father worked hard for a living too. He had the power of aloofness, which was considerable, and often the power of violence too. But this gave his son nothing to feed on. As we've said, Fifties' sons could only learn to 'act' like Dad and had none of his inner world to draw on. Problems arise, for instance, when this son goes into his own marriage. He has no masculine depth on which to draw – just the cardboard cutout of a silent father.

We can see a woman in a marriage, taking a stand on what matters to her, as being like the peak of a strong, solid pyramid of womanliness – since she stands on all the vast women's experience she has taken in. The man, taking a stand on what matters to him, has only a wobbly stack of single bricks – the sketchy, superficial examples of manliness he has cobbled together from movies, etc. So he is forever insecure and cannot deal on equal terms. He has never experienced the inside of men who shared themselves. He has only a grab-bag of cliches and gruff one-liners.

So, as often as not, he caves in or runs away or turns mean. I meet this continually in counselling: men who simply cannot be honest with their partners. It leads to enormous grief. Without confidence to put your case, nothing can be resolved. And confidence – for a man – comes from the father or from father-surrogates.

Getting it right!

For a start, it helps to show up in your own children's lives! During the pregnancy, if they hear your voice, often, they will soon distinguish it from their mother's and any other voices. They will turn to face you once they are born, recognising that familiar rumble. When they are small, hold them against you often and they will also *feel* your voice. A man's voice resonates deep in his chest and vibrates through a held baby, in a way they will come to love.

When you take them into your arms at birth, have your shirt open. Do not use soap, deodorant or scented cosmetics of any kind, so that they bond to the natural, clean, sweaty smell of you. Your unique odour signature will become reassuring to them.

Don't be separated from your wife and child in the hospital. Sleep in the room, care for the child so your wife can get some sleep. Of course, respect her wish to have time with the child alone too. Do not let nurses take your child to a nursery, when it can have its parents' own care. Organise some time off work for at least a month, or three if you can, so that the early days can be unhurried. Teach yourself to cook!

Watch for competitive feelings. On the cover of *Families and How to Survive Them* (John Cleese and Robyn Skinner's book on families), there is a cartoon of a man watching his wife breastfeed the baby. The man is sucking a dummy and looking most put out. When a new baby arrives, watch out for, and accept, competitive feelings if they arise. (They might not.) Your wife loves you, as well as the baby. But it's natural for her to switch, hormonally, to the kind of devotion that makes her able to care for the child and love doing it, in the first year. Support her, find a few minutes a day with her just to 'link up' and be patient. She'll come back to you!

Being there for your son

The Cleese-Skinner book, mentioned above, also includes a simple and profound cartoon in which a boy walks across a bridge, over a river, from his mother's side to his father's. This symbolises an essential stage in male development. As early as six or seven years of age, the primary identification of the boy must switch. He will love and relate intensely to his mother but he is not 'hers' any more. He actively wants to be with, and be like, his father. He can only do this if his father is around, available and interested in sharing time with him. This father needs to be doing things with him, enjoying sharing his life with him, challenging and testing him, but never wounding or belittling him. There are all kinds of forms that this can take.

Play-wrestling

> If you want to get along well with boys, you have to learn
> to wrestle.
>
> Paul Whyte

Children of both sexes love to get down on the floor and
play rough and tumble, be held in the air, be tickled, try
to pin your arms down, play games of all kinds. Boys who
feel secure will especially love their fathers or other men
to do this with them and they thrive on the competition of
matching strength and agility.

Several important and symbolic shifts are made in doing
this seemingly fun activity. The first is 'not hurting'. Inevitably, a child wrestling on the carpet will hurt an adult by
being too boisterous, not careful enough with an elbow or
a knee! If this happens, the father stops the action,
and says clearly to the boy, 'You can play-fight without
hurting. You're too precious and I'm too precious to be
hurt. Will you be careful while you are fighting not to hit
or hurt?'

The boy usually agrees. It will happen more than once,
of course, and be handled the same way. If it means
stopping because the child is just too hyped-up to exercise
self-control, then there's a lesson in this too. But the aim
is for them to learn how to fight without harm, to use lots
of strength but not hurt themselves or others.

A potent lesson is being learnt here. When the boy is
older, he will almost inevitably become stronger and larger
than his girlfriend or wife. He must know how to debate,
take criticism, experience strong emotions and, at the same
time, **never** use his physical strength to dominate or hurt
her. The restraint learned by actual wrestling will come in
handy in the verbal wrestling which all couples need to do
from time to time. *The boy learns to contain his strength,
from the example of a father who never hurts him and
who doesn't allow him to hurt others.*

Wrestling is, without doubt, a competition. This also carries an important symbolic message. This is that he is just a boy and not the boss. A father wrestles with his son sometimes *to win*. So the end point is (at least most of the time) the son getting pinned down, after a long, enjoyable struggle and 'giving in' – calling quits, admitting he lost. This takes balance. Winning shouldn't always be the aim. But if a boy is getting cocky, becoming a discipline problem, then often some play-fighting is more useful and (symbolically) more 'friendly' than a straight-out disciplinary action. The cue for this is when the boy uses something really trivial to provoke your attention and has a certain gleam in his eyes that says, 'Stop me, Dad!' It's especially needed by four- to six-year-olds, in our experience, but it doesn't stop there!

Winding-up and winding-down

Psychologist Jim Herzog first pointed out the unique pattern of play that fathers all over the world seem to demonstrate. I'm grateful to Alastair Spate, who described this pattern to me as follows:

> Imagine two parents on a living room floor with a two-year-old lad and a pile of blocks. The mother encourages the child to play with the blocks and at least construct a pile or some sort of rough structure. Typically, at some stage, the father will transform himself into a roaring monster-cum-bulldozer, knock over the bricks and provoke peals of delight in the child. From then, the two males 'wind up' in challenge and response, giggling and hooting, rivalling each other to make the biggest mess.
>
> When the father eventually senses some disapproval, or at least concern, in the mother, he begins to 'wind down' the play until a breathless equilibrium returns to the room and the boy rests in the arms of either of the parents.

This sort of play is very much the father's specialty. The crucial thing is the winding down. Here a father teaches his child, through play, the mastery of his energy and angers, sets the limits of aggression and how to stay in charge of one's emotions and not be flooded by them.

Most readers will have seen the uncontrolled inner and outer rages and depressions of the under-fathered boy, whose first experience of male limit-setting is likely to be the police, truant officer or warden in early adolescence – and by then he is literally a marked man. (Or marked and not yet a man.) He never learnt through this uniquely, fatherly play how to become the master in his own house of angers, dreams, yearnings and energy.

And you thought you were just playing! 'Winding oneself down' turns out to be a vital, life-saving skill – learned on the lounge-room floor or the back lawn. It frees you from being overtaken by your own emotions. This is the gift a good father can give.

Identifying an 'under-fathered' boy

Boys who are under-fathered can be diagnosed easily. They fall into two distinct types. One type takes on macho-mania: the wearing of aggressive clothes, collecting violent toys and comics or (if older) carrying knives and studying weapons and war obsessively. This type will usually group in highly competitive and low-quality friendships with other neglected boys or young men.

The other type is underconfident – a 'Mummy's boy' – and is often depressed. Younger boys of this type often have problems with bedwetting or soiling. They tend to get picked on at school, are reluctant to try new things or go to new places and often have irrational fears.

Both these types suffer from the same problem – father-hunger. Mothers will often not be able to fix these problems on their own. As their father, it's your job.

Discipline

In the bad old days, fathers were often the discipline 'bad guy' – the 'enforcer'. The fact that they were away from the house all day made them more scary. 'Wait till your father gets home!' was the somewhat malicious threat of exhausted and lonely mums.

Today, the scene is quite different. Wimpish fathers are everywhere. They leave discipline to their wives or, worse still, undermine them: 'Let the kids be – they aren't being that bad'; 'Just relax, honey, it doesn't really matter.' (Such men are in for a short marriage and a terrible sex life!)

Women and children need men to be at least equal partners in discipline. In fact, men have an actual talent for it. Boys especially require a certain good-natured combativeness in order to get the message through. Men who are comfortable with their masculinity enjoy this matching of strengths. They can do it without feeling threatened and without the same sense of exhaustion that women feel from being 'hard' on children. Somewhere, in their heart-of-hearts, mothers feel so loving to their children that they never want them to leave. Men, however, have a part of them that would like the kids to be gone yesterday! In a healthy marriage, partners compromise and give the children eighteen years and then nudge them out!

There is another reason why fathers need to take a tougher role. The feelings of a mother for her child are primarily tender, and the child reciprocates this. If a great deal of discipline is taking place from the mother, especially if it is negative and critical, a boy can start to feel that his mother hates him. Many mothers tell me, 'Every time I open my mouth, it's to criticise'. A boy can feel the mother-love eroding away. If the father is doing his bit, the mother relaxes, feels supported and is less cold or harsh as a result.

If the father 'takes on' the son – talks firmly and clearly about what is and isn't acceptable and if he reinforces this with nonviolent but firm follow-up – then the wife is able to relax and can remain more loving. This isn't to say the role division is all one way, but that the balance is skewed towards the father being harder. Both partners need to do both. In fact, unless the father also has a loving and involved role with his son or daughter, then his discipline will not work.

I've written a couple of books on the specifics of how to safely discipline children and teenagers which you may want to read. The essence is to get engaged, eyeball to eyeball, and be definite – so that children can state their case but are also made to listen to yours. This is quite the opposite of the techniques of isolation, star charts and mechanical means which Fifties' psychology turned up. Children do not need more remoteness. They need you to get involved.

Mother–son conflict

One of the most important of these developmental tasks, which a boy must successfully accomplish in order to achieve satisfying intimate relationships with women later in life, is that of separating emotionally from the mother.

The boy must come to experiences himself as profoundly independent of his mother – of her emotional states, of her needs, and of her sexual identity.

He can accomplish these difficult tasks ... most success-fully when he has a strong, and present, father or other idealized male in his life. In the absence of such men, even good-enough mothers are frighteningly overwhelming to the fragile gender-specific emerging self-structures of boys.

Douglas Gillette in *Wingspan*

There is a turning point around the age of fourteen for boys which can be summed up in a single example. Many boys at this age, without consciously knowing why, start to have problems with their mother. The son knows deep down he must break free from her. Driven by this pressure, he may act ugly, be lazy, rude, even menacing to her. This should never be allowed to proceed. The father, hearing this start to happen (from behind his paper in the lounge room!) goes into the kitchen where son and mother are 'squaring off'. He intervenes:

'What did you just say to your mother?' He waits for an answer. Then he continues:

'You need to **always** talk to your mother with respect. You can argue, but don't ever be disrespectful or threaten her. If you do, you will have me to deal with.' (This isn't to say he will get physical, just being there is enough.)

He then allows the pair to continue the discussion. He may join in, but his role is not to take over for his wife – just ensure courtesy and respect. This isn't to imply that his wife can't take care of herself, only that she shouldn't, in balance, need to.

Having an adequate father in the house makes a huge difference.You can pick at a glance those women who feel backed up by their husbands in the home. They are glowing, relaxed, warm and feminine. Women who have to do all the hard stuff – argue with the builder, battle the kids and make the decisions – look hard and tired. These women deserve better.

But all over the country now, one sees hulking sons acting ugly in the kitchen and talking rudely to their mothers, and I think it's an attempt to make themselves unattractive. If the old men haven't done their work to interrupt the mother–son unity, what else can the boys do to extricate themselves but to talk ugly? It's quite unconscious, and there's no elegance in at all.

A clean break from the mother is crucial, but it's simply

not happening. This doesn't mean that the women are doing something wrong. I think the problem is the older men are not really doing their job.

Robert Bly

A mentor for your son

Even the best fathers cannot raise their sons alone. Fathers need extra help from other men to do this properly. In a houseful of boisterous and defiant sons, more manpower is needed. In tribal situations the whole male community got involved with the teenage boys – mentoring, training and initiating them. A father could count on all kinds of help, and boys could count on positive input – usually more relaxed and accepting than fathers manage to be.

A boy in his mid to late teens needs other men to step in who will teach him skills, give him a sense of worth and take him out beyond the family walls. In other words, he moves to a mentor. His own father may be a mentor to someone else's son. Different from fathering, mentoring is an informing but less-nurturing role, which in no way takes away from or threatens the closeness of father and son. In the old days, this was the person who taught a boy his craft for life. This old arrangement took the heat out of the father-son relationship, which can get very tense, as anyone who has taught their teenager to drive will know!

In practice this means a few simple steps. If you have sons, you also need to have groups of male friends whom they can be around, so that they feel accepted into the adult male world. You don't then need to be 'into' sport, fishing, computers and so on, unless you choose to. There will be others who can step into this quite naturally. There will always be deeply intellectual fathers with athletic and extrovert sons, and vice versa. This needn't be a problem if the father is willing to allow and encourage good men from amongst his acquaintances who can supplement what he offers and thereby create a balanced adolescent experience.

> A boy needs help to learn about his own gifts and identity, and help to learn how to identify someone who has mastered the skills that are the birthright of his nature. With so many life options to choose from, our boys could actually use a mentor in the very process of finding a mentor.
> Their lives seldom expose them to mature men doing things of such quality as to inspire a boy's emulation and his willingness to discipline himself in anticipation of being ready for his own chance later in life. In this light, we should not be surprised that our teenagers have grown apathetic about preparing for roles that are either invisible to them or that exercise no charm over their imaginations.
>
> John Palmour in *Wingspan*

Wise men understand that the myriad activity groups around which people organise their leisure time serve a more important purpose. A fishing club isn't really about fishing, or a cricket club about cricket (though part of the role involves treating these things as being of extraordinary importance!). They are really just ways that men can care for each other and take boys into tutelage, give them positive messages and so provide a vehicle for character growth and maturation. (This is often misunderstood and so the point of the activity is lost – for instance, in competitive sport which actually encourages violence on the field, or the use of steroids, etc.) But for the most part, these groups are our substitute tribes and are essential to a healthy society.

What single mothers can do

Single mothers are usually very alert to the need for male models for their sons. Once they find a way to supplement this need, many problems of young sons – such as over-shyness or over-aggressiveness – disappear. There is a lot you can do if you are a single mother of boys. Visit your sons' school and ask if they can have a male teacher next year. Choose the athletic, musical, scouting avenues that have good men in them. Be choosy. Select on the basis of, 'Are these the kind of men I want my son to turn into?' That is what role model means. Be careful – sometimes sexually abusive men prey on fatherless boys, exploiting their craving for male affection.

Despite the risks, boys need men – as the following story illustrates dramatically.

A mother in a ToughLove group (a form of self-help group for embattled parents) told the group how her fourteen-year-old son would simply not get out of bed and go to school in the mornings. Several men from her group offered to go, as a team, and rouse her son from bed and off to school each morning. This they did.

Imagine the boy's surprise! After a couple of visits, they only had to be 'on call'. The boy got his act together. He protested but he also seemed kind of pleased.

Single mothers can raise boys well, but not alone. They have to have the help of a wider network. Their self-care skills must be honed to avoid negativity or flying off the handle, yet maintain good discipline – especially around the mid teens. 'It takes a village to raise a child' – and raising boys takes women *and* men.

Fathers with daughters

Daughters need some special things from fathers. One of these is affirmation. This means the feeling of being flattered, admired but never invaded or exploited – so that they can practise conversation and mutual admiration with a 'safe' male. Through talking with their fathers and other older men, daughters can gain assurance, feel worthwhile and know that they do not 'need' the first beau that comes their way. A realistic understanding of male qualities and male foibles is priceless for a girl.

The quality of her mother's and father's relationship is important to a girl. Knowing that her father aligns with her mother at a deep level, and can't be seduced or undermined, means that she recognises boundaries. She learns how to say 'no' and take 'no' for an answer. If Mum and Dad get on well, she will want *at least* that quality of relationship in her own marriage.

Fathers of teenage daughters will naturally feel some protectiveness and jealousy. If this is moderate, it will work quite well. It doesn't hurt for boyfriends to be moderately terrified! Some clear safety limits can be set, appropriate for the daughter's age and stage. A friend of mine who is divorced from his first wife, learnt that his thirteen-year-old daughter was at a party with some people who were far beyond her depth to deal with. He quickly gathered two large, male friends, and went and got her. She made a token complaint, but was basically very relieved.

Being trustworthy is something a teenager has to prove – it isn't a right. At the same time, a father has to guard against being jealous out of his own need. He needs to envisage his daughter moving out, being strong in making her own choices, having a happy life. No-one will ever be good enough for her, but luckily it isn't his choice!

Defending and protecting

Men have to protect their children adequately. To a boy, a father should represent strength and protection. For some little boys this can be a crucial role.

Sean, aged nine, had been in boarding school for only two weeks when the principal called him into his office, locked the door and began to sexually abuse him. The principal gave dire threats to the boy should he ever tell anyone. The abuse continued on a weekly basis through that term.

When his father visited the school at the end of term, the principal met with him to discuss Sean's progress. Sean came in to the office and immediately took in the scene. The powerful monster-principal, smug at his desk; his father, without a chair to sit on, was perched on a woodbox beside the hearth. Immediately Sean knew that his father had no power or confidence in this place. He felt (rightly or wrongly) that his father could offer no protection. He spoke nothing of the events to his father, who left oblivious. Sean remembers to this day the smile the principal gave him as his father departed. The abuse continued all that year.

Men need protection. Robert Bly speaks angrily about the abuse of young men by the generals in Vietnam. These twenty-year-olds, often with idealistic or religious backgrounds, found themselves immersed in bloodshed, horror and the ambiguity of Vietnam. Their father-figure generals then sent them to the brothels of Thailand to 'let off steam' – destroying their feeling for womanhood or tenderness, completing their disillusionment with life. (As a result of the conduct of this war, veteran suicides now far exceed the death toll in the entire conflict.)

At any age men, through their isolation, can be extraordinarily vulnerable. A nurse friend of mine came across an old man in tears in the stairwell of a hospital. He told her the problem – he was to have his tongue surgically cut out that day, because it was cancerous. She talked with him for a time. At the end of the conversation, he had decided to cancel the surgery. He wished to live out his life – he was eighty-four – with his ability to speak, and taste, intact. He might die sooner, but he would die an intact human being.

Shielding young men from soul assaults

There are many assaults on the souls of men, and they begin early. Some women hate all men and will see in male children an avenue of revenge. The son of a friend of mine went for his first day at school. He was, and is, a talkative, sparrow-like little boy – full of life. The young female teacher became angry at his chattiness, half an hour into the first school lesson of his life. She told him to stand by the waste-bin in the corner. He didn't hear her correctly – he thought she said *in* the waste-bin – and so that is what he did. She let him stay there for ten minutes, occasionally ridiculing him to the class.

Unless boys are protected, how else can they keep their tender feelings intact? Unless we bring a nurturing fierceness to our lives, how can we ever heal? When men's leader Michael Meade speaks to audiences of men, he often reads pieces of poetry from around the world. As he reads, men begin quietly weeping. Soon whole groups are crying openly and profoundly, like floodgates opening. I have often seen the same thing in men's programs that I have taught. Not for centuries have men in our culture been so open. Something very good and important is beginning to happen.

Protecting your son's sexual development

If you have teenage sons, it's probably a good idea to let them lock their bedroom doors and sleep in privacy. Then they can relax! As mentioned earlier, a sensuous and accepting attitude to masturbation is needed, in order for boys to learn to be relaxed lovers. The chance to read and see quality erotica – material that shows men and women in equal and enjoyable contact – will help. Never force, invade or push sexuality on children. Simply allow their natural interest and natural sense of privacy to be there. Boys will probably obtain 'girlie' magazines and pictures, but these shouldn't be plastered on walls or bought with your permission or your money! Much of this material is sexist, phony and deceptive in it's role-modelling. Let your sons know it's okay to admire women's bodies but always to see women as people.

Avoiding cheapness

Our society's induction of boys into the world of sex would make one weep. What we teach boys about sex is far from sacred. It's mostly just cheap. But as a father or mother we can take a sword to this cheapness.

There's a scene in the movie, *The Rose*, where the heroine, beautifully played by Bette Midler, is a blowsy, addicted, past-her-prime rock singer. In one critical scene she is waiting in a recording studio along with some country musicians. She bats her eyes at a young man in Western shirt, who looks about eighteen, and he responds, albeit awkwardly. She is about to move into major flirting mode when the boy's father walks into the room, sees what is happening and cuts her dead. 'Don't try that cheap slut behaviour with my son', he tells her (or words to that effect).

It's a jolting moment in the film, and it takes the wind out of her sails too. It seems like a body blow to her whole self-image. Not because of the criticism *per se*, but **because she knows, that the father is right**. He is a musician too, but out of a different mould – a craftsman, clean cut and straight backed – and he has named a wrong. What she was doing was on one level harmless, even flattering, to the young man. On another level it was ambiguous, uncaring, a female form of sexual harassment.

Boys need to understand that girls are capable of misusing them, that a penis can be a handle to get dragged around by! A female office worker in her late teens, interviewed on Bettina Arndt's courageous documentary, 'When "No" Means "Maybe"', illustrated this perfectly. She talked gaily about the pleasure of getting her dates sexually overheated, only to turn them down. It was a game, played for the power buzz it gave her, and she saw no reason to be ashamed. She spoke for only two minutes, but when she had finished the 'all men are bastards' position lay in tatters. Clearly *some* men act like bastards, some *women* act like bitches, and teenagers of both genders have to be wary.

What if your son is gay?

For some parents, the normal concerns about sexuality are complicated by the discovery that one of their offspring is gay. Having a homosexual son or daughter can cause pain because it interrupts all the forward fantasies we hold for our children. The question 'why?' is often a source of torment, which is quite needless. The research on sexual preferences is strongly leaning towards the die being cast while a baby is still in the womb – and that certain hormonal switching in the brain at this time leads to a young person being gay or lesbian. It's felt by some re-searchers that in a proportion of young people the die is not set, and that they can literally 'go either way'. In these cases, family dynamics may play a role. The combination which therapists feel is most likely to make a young man become gay is a remote, critical father, and an over-involved mother. However, millions of young men have this combi-nation but do not become gay. Nonetheless, there is a quality in many gay relationships of young men seeking in their lover the father who never loved them. This can lead to immature relationships, just as it does in many straight couples.

When it's all boiled down, the concerns of parents of gay teenagers are just the same as the concerns of any parent. They want their son to have a happy life. They hope that he will handle his sexuality in a responsible and self-respecting way. And they hope that he will find a stable partnership if this is his wish.

Sex, whatever form it takes, is still basically a beautiful and God-given thing. Young gay people discovering their sexuality need acceptance and understanding. They also need a wider society which is not homophobic or persecutory – where healthy role-models of gay people are out in the open making good lives for themselves. It's tough enough being a teenager without being in a persecuted minority. Needless to say the Men's Movement is firmly in favour of gay men's – and lesbian women's – rights and value as members of mainstream society.

Affirming the sacredness of sex

The urge to conceal details of human sexuality from children may not have been prudishness at all, not in the first place. Perhaps it comes from a more ancient tradition – that it is one of the world's most powerful forms of magic and not to be trivialised by passing into childish hands. There are other lessons that should come first – simple things like how to be good friends, how to respect other people, know about consequences and to combine passion with carefulness. Ideally, sexual experience should be earned – as it was in many cultures through various tests and stages – and its power preserved until one has the maturity to handle it.

We must find out how to teach boys and girls that they are sacred, that their sexuality is godlike (which includes wild, lustful and healthy) just as all other parts of their lives and actions are divine. Perhaps we need a little more Norman Lindsay and a little less of Doctor Ruth!

Sometimes Christian sex education succeeds far better than the secular forms which aim to be value-free and just end up mechanical. Religious views at least emphasise the joy of sex and some kind of sacred context in which it takes place. Sexual reserve is different to prudery – it is a wish for there to be more than just awkwardness and rush. Large numbers of young people report their early sexual experiences to be confusing and disillusioning. Luckily, we usually don't give up!

Abandoned sons are waiting for their fathers

Today there are millions of mothers raising sons without a man in the house. This can work, and work well, but the odds are against it – for the reasons we have already given. As a separated father, or a father relinquishing a child for adoption, the thing to remember is that somewhere your son is waiting, with all kinds of mixed feelings, to know you and know your side of the story. If the hostility between you and his mother is an obstacle, then you should work to drop this on your part. Let him know that you are available, and ready when he is able to sort things out.

Sometimes a son living with his mother will unconsciously start to make it so difficult for her that she will consider letting him go to his father. On occasions, to everyone's surprise, this can be just the right thing for 'finishing off' a young man's development. If a father sidesteps this responsibility his soul will be wounded. Some separated fathers refuse to acknowledge their children in any way. Many fathers just vanish from the family scene following a divorce. Since this is most likely done from a position of hurt – out of hostility to the mother – then it is very unjust to the child. A father has the power to bless his children's lives and the power to greatly damage them, depending on whether he maintains or loses contact. For men there is, potentially, enormous satisfaction and peace of mind if you take on your proper role here – and being a good father can compensate for the feelings of failure in divorce. Some men have told me they only got close to their children after they divorced their wives.

Fatherless children

As I was finishing this chapter, a new and impressive book arrived in the mail, called *Fatherless America*. The author,

David Blankenhorn, summarises in a clear and very scholarly way what is known worldwide about the effects on kids of having no fathers available in their homes or in their lives.

This book is something of a breakthrough. For some time now, it has been almost accepted that fathers were unnecessary, and perhaps even a health hazard to children. Much of the social work literature pushed the idea that children might be better off without those nasty males around. And many people made life choices based on such beliefs. Nowadays, in America, half of all children will spend time in a fatherless home.

According to Blankenhorn, this astonishing disappearance of men from the family scene may be the key to most of our social problems. For while some fathers have certainly been child-abusers, wife-beaters, drunkards and deadbeats, the vast majority are not and never have been. The research is clear – kids with dads are better off. Here are just a few of the findings.

Boys and girls both have greater self-esteem if their fathers are still in the home. They do better in school, stay on in school longer, become more qualified and are more likely to be employed. Children with fathers in the home are less likely to be sexually abused, less likely to have trouble with the law and less likely to be beaten up. Girls are less likely to be raped or experience early sexual behaviour or teenage pregnancy.

Daughters without fathers are more 'malleable' and adapted to pleasing men than are daughters who are secure in a father's love and respect. Boys with no fathers, or with fathers who are not around much, are much more likely to be violent, to get into trouble, to do poorly in schools, and to be a member of a teenage gang in adolescence. Families without a man are usually poorer, and children of these families are more likely to move down rather than up the socioeconomic ladder. The greatest threat to children's safety is the 'boyfriend father'. A pregnant woman is four times more likely to be assaulted by a boyfriend than by a husband.

None of the above is to say that a bad marriage shouldn't end, or that any father is better than none. What is does say, quite incontrovertibly, is that children's lives are much, much better given a half-decent man who is the biological father or a committed step-dad, who lives in the home or is close by and deeply involved.

Early in my fathering career, I thought that I was just an accessory in my children's lives, a bit of light entertainment for them – my partner's helpmate in parenting. I assumed that the best sort of father was a kind of imitation mother. What's more, it suited me to retreat to the safe and manageable world of work, where I was usually successful and respected, as opposed to the messiness and risk of taking young children shopping or being stuck inside with toddlers on a rainy day!

Now I see my job as being equal to that of my partner. I have become more comfortable and challenged by the role of being a dad – my life is so much happier. I do not (and this is very important) spend time with my children out of a sense of guilt or obligation, but because it feeds my soul and is a job I am proud of doing well. I often feel painfully unprepared for the job, and I frequently 'get it wrong'. I am committed to finding out how to father well, by consulting with my partner, by reading and, especially, by talking to other men about how they are doing it.

Fathering is a vital, honourable and essential part of the fabric of human life. And it's time we acknowledged that.

In a nutshell

1 Flush out of your brain the old models:

- the father as an arrogant king;
- the father as a judge;
- the father as a passive blob; and
- the father who is hardly ever there.

2 Acknowledge the fact that boys need fathers around many hours a day. *Do stuff with your son.* The path to closeness with sons is activity together. But be sure to talk too.

3 Get involved from pregnancy onwards. You can be a presence in his life even in the womb, as a baby, as a little child and so on.

4 Wrestle with your children. Teach your boys, through wrestling, to show care and how to be a good loser or winner. Help them to be excited and also teach them when to calm down.

5 Be a firm but safe disciplinarian. Back up your wife and learn firm-love techniques. (My book, *More Secrets of Happy Children*, focuses on this.)

6 Be involved with daughters too. Admire them, teach them self-sufficiency. Respect their space and never evaluate their looks, except positively.

7 Protect your sons from the violent, the shoddy and the pseudo-tough – and from having their feelings hurt or hardened over.

8 Help to make other men available for your son to learn from and be admired by. Create all-male recreation on at least an annual basis. Think about forms of initiation which will be positive and memorable as a spiritual launching of your sons into adolescence and then manhood.

Other voices

- The average father looks out from behind his newspaper fifty percent less than he did a decade ago!

  Robert Bly

- Dorothy Dinnerstein, professor of psychology at Rutgers University, has developed a theory that links greater male violence and lack of empathic nurturing qualities, with the fact that boys are reared almost exclusively by women ... It receives considerable corroboration from diverse and independent findings in the social sciences.

  Psychological studies of families in which child-rearing is shared by the parents, or in which the father is the primary caretaker, reveal that the sons in these families are more empathic than boys raised in the traditional way. In a twenty-six-year longitudinal study of empathy, researchers found that the single factor most highly linked to empathic concern was the level of paternal involvement in child care.

  Myriam Miedzian in *Boys Will Be Boys*

- He feels powerless out in this world, so he attacks something that is safe, something that can't attack him back. And one of the best targets he can find, especially, is a little son. If the son is feeling powerful, is spontaneous, full of life, what do you think that does to a man who's numb? It threatens him, and he has to squash it.'

  Marvin Allen

- Sometimes sons will try to activate their own emotional bodies through rock music, or gang activity, but it does not succeed. A woman who notices that a man's emotional body is not activated will sometimes offer to activate it for him by helping him to express his feelings or teaching him to be more sensual. It may be that sex deepens the integration of physical and emotional body in a woman, but the same thing doesn't seem to work for a man. In general, I would say that the emotional body of a man cannot be activated by a woman. That's the job of old men. In some cultures, the older men give years and years of their lives to just that.

Robert Bly

• The traditional male harness has meant the early and often premature establishment of career, marriage and family, which gave the man the appearance of maturity but actually made genuine self-development very difficult, because he was constantly struggling to deal with external pressures.

Herb Goldberg in *The New Male*

• Our fathers traded their bodies for money to show they were men. Our mothers traded their bodies for security and protection. They 'took care of' our dads, and our dads 'took care of' our moms. I almost never saw my dad treat my mom as an equal. I almost never saw my mom treat my dad that way either. Either Dad treated her like a daughter or mother, or Mom treated him like a son or her dad. He pointed his body towards hers, she towards his, and yet somehow for me there was No-Body at home.

Men are beginning to believe that they are some-body, and that while they can't be everything to every-body, they can be more open and more honest with themselves and the ones they love.

John Lee in *At My Father's Wedding*

Men Raising Children

... when psychiatrist Kyle Pruett began his study of children raised by their fathers, he was somewhat sceptical as to whether these children would do as well on the Yale Developmental Schedule as those from traditional families. (The Schedule enables researchers to record progress in a young child's motor functions, language, social skills and ability to solve problems.) He was shocked to find that these children were doing better in all areas. While he speculates as to a number of reasons why they did so well, he concludes that the most likely reason is that these children had two highly involved parents. The mothers were fully committed to their children's well-being and growth, even though they had full-time jobs outside the home. In the traditional family, the father is not usually as intensely involved with the children.

One-third of the men in Pruett's group became primary nurturers, not out of any desire to do so but for purely practical reasons, and often as an interim measure – until a wife who was ill came out of hospital or until they could get a job. They then continued far longer than anticipated. This makes Pruett's book of particular interest.

Typical of a number of men in the group is Mr Blue, who says, 'I love looking after my son. But I would never have guessed it. In fact, if my high-school jock buddies ever knew I was doing it, they'd fall over dead from laughing.'

Pruett tells us that the 'clearest change over time had occurred in those fathers who'd been economically forced into the primary-parent role, and who were often initially quite anxious, if not unhappy, with their lot. They thawed most slowly to their task, but ... their children were indistinguishable from the "early choosers" by age two.'

Pruett explains this in terms of the father's 'engrossment' with his child. The father who connects with his child at a very early age, who participates in the nurturing of the child, forms a deep emotional bond which seems to elude most traditional fathers.

Myriam Miedzian in *Boys Will Be Boys*

• Hilda and Seymour Parker, at the University of Utah, did a comparative study of fifty-six men who were known to have sexually abused their minor daughters, and fifty-four men with no known child sexual-abuse in their backgrounds. They found a very significant corellation between lack of involvement in childcare, and nurturance, and child abuse. The authors conclude that it is quite possible that 'if the primary childcare were shared more equally by men and women, one basis for ... the sexual exploitation of females might be eliminated'.

Myriam Miedzian

8
Making School Good for Boys

Each morning, if the weather was fine, the man used to walk his six-year-old son to school. They lived in a quiet country town, and it was a beautiful downhill walk. The boy would skip and run about, pointing out birds, insect life, ripening blackberries.

As they drew closer to the school, though, a curious change always came over the boy. A change which saddened the father, for he knew what it was. The boy's voice deepened, his shoulders tensed up, his face got serious. He was putting on the armour all males (in this culture) feel they must wear.

After parents, the next biggest influence on boys' quality of life is the world of school. We have suddenly begun to realise that school is not good for boys – at least not in the way it is currently being conducted.

The work of NSW MP Stephen O'Doherty awoke many in the education scene to the fact that boys were going backwards in school. O'Doherty talks movingly to audiences about his own experiences of being bullied as a child. His 1994 report into the need for a boys' education strategy in NSW serves as a blueprint for school reform.

We have known for some time that coeducational schools

disadvantage girls in certain ways, such as by limiting their choices of subjects and by reducing their involvement in the class through physical intimidation and domination of the classroom by some boys. The girls' equity movement in schools has to continue well into the future so that our daughters have a productive and fair chance at school and in life.

What we didn't realise until recently was that school also is a bad place for boys. Boys do more poorly than girls in exams and have lower retention rates (leaving school earlier). Also, the emotional environment of the boys' world of school is often intimidating and negative.

Professor Ken Rigby, an expert on bullying, has found that one in five boys gets bullied at school at least once per week. A boy who has had a gentle and cooperative start in life at home may find that to be accepted he has to put on macho pretensions, act mean, disparage girls and even join in acts of bullying.

Rigby describes the pattern in which the boy who is not academically bright (or is not helped to be so) becomes humiliated and angered in the classroom, and recovers his standing through bullying others in the schoolyard. This is not unfamiliar to most men in their recollections of boyhood – even episodes of 'The Simpsons' portray this accurately. Professor Rigby stresses the need for a non-blame approach, which does not further alienate. This by no means implies being soft on bullying. Research on effective school programs has shown that every instance must be confronted, and the playground be made a safe place by teacher presence. The difference is that the problem is solved, and the needs of individual boys resolved, so they can move beyond bullying behaviour.

He believes that the cold and uncaring nature of staff–student interaction contributes to the bullying atmosphere in a school. The staff bully the children, who bully other children! The more aggressive the staff, the less warm and involved the principal and other teachers, the more likely the children will be to harm each other.

The patterns of violence are very predictable in boys' lives. It's known that men who hit their wives or children, or who end up in prison for habitual violence, were easily diagnosable by mid-primary school. A recent study found that a very high proportion of boys who behaved aggressively in primary school went on to become drink drivers – often being charged with this offence before actually gaining a driving licence. Richard Fletcher (of the University of Newcastle) points to the statistics showing that a young man who dies in a road accident, on average, takes the lives of at least one and often two others with him – usually girl passengers. When boys' development is ignored, everyone reaps the harm.

Sport – a disaster area for body and soul

Sport is also a focus of much damage at school. In a 1994 rugby match between two prestigious schools in Queensland, a young man took a punch at an opposing player. The other boy hit back, striking the side of the first player's head. The blow was fatal. The enormous grief, loss and horror of this young man's death (for all the boys involved), was directly attributable to neither of these youngsters, but to the 'ethos' and 'hype' generated by adults around a children's sport. (There are similarities in the child-abuse of girl gymnasts that passes for training.) The adults involved in school sport load the honour of the school (and all kinds of pressures) onto young boys, who should be just enjoying themselves, and this invites tragedy. It's known that boys' testosterone levels increase when they are placed in ongoing situations of threat and danger, and that this leads to even more aggressive behaviour.

Some coaches today urge boys in contact sports to hit and hurt 'as long as they can get away with it'. These are not honourable men and should be deeply shamed for providing such poor leadership. Sydney academic Dr Peter

West believes that sport is one of the primary sources of shaping a defective masculine image – arrogant, elitist, violent, unfeeling, individualistic, competitive and less than fully human. (The boy as a robot.) For this reason, many parents have become deeply ambivalent about sport – for its physical as well as psychological dangers. Yet sport can be so positive in a boy's life, given the right conditions.

The problems can be summed up in the following ways. Boys today, already underfathered, and beginning to show problem behaviour, come into a school environment that is largely feminine. They fit in poorly, and tend to form an anti-school subculture. When they do meet male role-models, usually later in school, these men may not always possess fatherly or nurturing qualities themselves. It can be the damaged leading the damaged.

Against this tide work many superb and understanding women and men who love boys and see their potential. School can, and does, provide a way for boys to be socialised and grow into adulthood assisted by resources far beyond those which the family can offer alone. We have to get more men into schools, and they must be the right kind of men. And we have to strengthen the programs that help boys become caring and aware human beings, to understand their gender dynamics and to relate comfortably and respectfully with girls.

Seven steps to school reform

Seven key areas of school reform have been identified by groups of teachers and principals (lead by myself and Rex Stoessiger) in schools around the country. These are as follows.

1 Male teachers available at all levels of schooling

Right now, in almost all levels of schooling (especially in primary schools), the great majority of teachers are female. Many schools have no men in them at all. At the same time, many boys (perhaps as many as one in three) have no male figures at home and no men active in their lives. School is their last chance to get some surrogate fathering or mentoring. It's very striking to realise that over eighty percent of nonreaders and problem learners are boys. We can speculate as to whether this is a direct consequence of the *inadvertent femininity of schools*. Boys need role models who can show them that learning is a masculine activity, that men are interested in them, and are not always remote, critical or uncaring. This may be their only chance to experience men who are nonviolent, friendly, good at dealing with misbehaviour and interested in their development. Men can show boys that the world of reading, writing, music, art and learning is as much a man's as a woman's world.

One option would be to legislate for recruitment and staffing changes, to guarantee that all boys (and girls) have access to at least one in three teachers being male during their primary years. (Female teachers displaced from schools could be promoted to correct the imbalance higher up in the system!) This would vastly improve the success of education for boys *and* girls and alleviate a significant proportion of schooling and later-life problems. Such policies are being implemented now in the U.S. specifically for black youngsters.

2 A change in the role of male principals

Most principals are men. This should not be so and needs redressing. For the time being, if the principal is a man – and often the only man in the school – it is important that he is accessible for and interactive with the children. He should not be remote, hidden behind administrative roles or continually taken away from school by other demands. Like it or not, he is a father-figure and needs to be a good one.

3 More boyish modes of learning

A lot of school's learning requirements are female oriented. Schools require and reward quiet, cooperative, verbal, fine-motor, indoor, artistic and passive kinds of activity. There is clear evidence from many studies that boys develop their fine-motor skills more slowly than girls in early primary school. They feel stupid and awkward if expected to produce the same kind of work at the same age. Whether these differences are cultural or conditioned, the result is known to every teacher. With very few exceptions, girls take to education more easily. Boys often bridle at, and have difficulty fitting in to, a classroom regime and carrying out classroom activities.

Education for boys needs to emphasise movement, vigour and going beyond four walls. They need more exciting or natural activity, which utilises male qualities instead of repressing them. This should not be limited to sport but extended to science, art, music, reading, maths, etc. It should be said that many of these change would benefit girls too. None of these recommendations aims at restricting either sex, but in expanding the breadth of offerings to both.

4 Releasing women teachers from the need to fight with problem boys

The Men's Movement traces many problems of boys – especially violence and misbehaviour – to an unconscious expression of father-hunger. By playing up, boys and young men are showing their need to be engaged, valued and disciplined by strong, loving male figures.

Female teachers often have horrendous, fruitless struggles with 'high-need' boys who have little respect for women and who prevent the whole class from learning in the meantime. Even the most effective and experienced female teachers have told us they feel the boys are needing – virtually asking for – something that they, as women, cannot offer. They can achieve a truce, a feeling of respect, but still feel that these boys and young men need something more.

Women teachers should **not** have to struggle continually with boys who need something they cannot provide. They should get much better back-up and be relieved of being at 'the sharp end' with troubled boys. Such boys should be especially targeted for male attention. This should not be just punitive attention but preventive and long-term involvement aimed at giving them a positive, masculine self-image.

5 Training of male teachers in the mentor role

Boys need men – but not just any men. Readers will recall their own schooldays when more men worked in primary education and how many of these men were maladjusted (and even sadistic) individuals. Today many male teachers can be more interested in the career track than the genuine needs of children. Concerted help is needed to develop mentoring skills in teachers and to help them understand the ancient position of caring for the spirit, as well as the memory banks, of their students.

Male teachers may be poor role models because they have never received the mentoring which they now need to impart. Special training is needed. In particular:

- training in human development and in counselling and conflict resolution;
- understanding how boys lacking affection will often develop aggression as a substitute;
- meeting father-hunger in boys with no father – appropriate ways to care for fatherless boys;
- the hero-or-villain dynamic in young men – how to redirect energies in constructive ways;
- 'tough love' confronting skills – how to teach thinking and problem solving as a means of discipline.

6 Use of male–female teaching teams

Many boys and girls have never seen men and women working together and doing so successfully. Male and female co-principals, teaching teams and married couples as teachers should be encouraged. These will be the only opportunities many children have to see men and women treating each other with respect and acting cooperatively.

7 Gender equity programs – for boys too

Many good feminist teachers manage to be committed to the advancement of girls and support and encourage boys as well. Yet mothers have told us that they feel their sons as young as kindergarten age are being made to feel inferior, just for being boys. Boys can be a problem, but they do not just wilfully **choose** to be difficult, lacking in social skills or aggressive, etc. Boys get trapped, just as much as girls do, in low self-esteem and maladaptive behaviour. The difference is that their ways of showing this are more of a problem to others. Some feminist teachers would say, 'More attention for boys – why should they get any more special attention?' But the fact is, if we want to solve the problems, we have to work from both ends. Most girls will want to know boys, will marry men and work with men. Things won't improve for girls unless boys are helped to make the corresponding changes.

Specific programs for boys, run by male-affirming men and women, are needed to equip boys with the skills to stay alive and be competent socially, at school, at work, as husbands and as fathers. Boys need to learn fathering and the care of younger children throughout their schooling. Peer support and cross-age tutoring are good examples. Boys themselves appreciate the programs and there are measurable benefits to behaviour.

In conclusion

To our pleasure and relief the reaction from **women** teachers to all seven of these ideas has been overwhelmingly positive. They have told us, 'Yes, this accurately describes what has been missing', 'We **do** have to do something about boys, to complement what is starting to happen with girls' and ' Thank goodness we now have some possible answers'.

Rather than endlessly playing 'more disadvantaged than thou' between the genders, we can recognise that boys and girls need different kinds of help. Schools, at present, by treating all students the same, aren't being fair to either gender.

Implementing just a few of the measures discussed above would create an improvement in the lot of boys, and before long would be bringing a better kind of young man out into the wider society.

In a nutshell

School can often be a place of fear and failure for boys. We can make school more boy-friendly in the following ways:

1 Making the playground environment safer by stopping bullying and violence by either pupils or teachers.

2 Recruiting more of the right kind of men, especially into primary education.

3 Stopping over-competitiveness in sport, and reinventing sport for enjoyment, self-development and exercise – not for the glory of the few.

4 Helping teachers develop a co-parenting and mentoring role in boys' emotional development (so that school is an extension of family, and the 'whole boy' is the focus and aim).

9
Finding a Job with Heart

Men love to work. Late in the evening if you drive through working men's suburbs, you will always see garage lights on. Inside, groups of men labour over old cars, lovingly modifying, repairing and maintaining late into the night. Others are busy building furniture in their workshops or working in metal and wood. These are mostly men who have worked hard all day in uninteresting jobs but who, with passion and intelligence, apply themselves at night-time to their real interests. Among the middle classes, the focus shifts to 'renovating' – that endless fixing-up of our dwellings that seems to fill the whole of the years from twenty-five to fifty – before we give up and slide downhill again! In other countries, (England, for instance) a plethora of exotic and weird hobbies – from electric trains to rose breeding, guinea pigs to Shakespearean acting – seem to draw men out from the stifling ordinariness of their daytime lives.

Comradeship

In her remarkable book, *The Continuum Concept*, Jean Liedloff describes a group of Amazon Indian men dragging a dugout canoe up a series of waterfalls. It takes hours. Suddenly, as they grunt their way up the last rapids, one man slips and the heavy canoe slams against the others and is shot by the force of the water hundreds of metres back down the cascade. The men laugh uproariously, though several have big bruises and cuts. Still chuckling and ribbing each other, they climb down the slippery rocks to start over again. Liedloff marvels at the resilience of spirit of Amazon men and women, at the attitude they all seem to share, and wonders how such optimism is trained into their children.

> We know that for hundreds of thousands of years, men have admired each other, and been admired by women in particular, for their *activity*. Men and women alike once called on men to pierce the dangerous places, carry handfuls of courage to the waterfalls, dust the tails of the wild boars. All knew that if men did that well, the women and the children could sleep safely. *(Now everything has changed.)* The activity men were once loved for is not required.
>
> Men have been loved for their astonishing initiative, embarking on wide oceans, starting a farm in rocky country, imagining a new business, doing it skilfully, working with beginnings, doing what has never been done. Young Viking men sometimes trained themselves by walking on the ends of the oars while the rowers continued rowing.
>
> Robert Bly

Working hard, and enjoying it, comes naturally to men. Yet it has been somewhat debased. D.H. Lawrence described how, in industrial England, the men working in the coal mines took satisfaction and found comradeship in their work and were proud of being good providers. Then schooling was introduced and, rather than working with their fathers, the boys began going to school. There they were taught by white-collared teachers that their fathers' world – the sweaty, difficult world of physical labour – was demeaning and that by applying themselves they (the young

FINDING A JOB WITH HEART   **153**

boys) could aspire to a clean, educated, 'higher' world. The fact that this 'advancement' meant an adult life spent stooped at desks doing dreary clerical tasks by quill pen was not really questioned. One was 'bettering oneself'. There was something virtuous in being clean, in never exerting one's body.

Fit to be tied

Powerful symbols soon divided men. One of these was the necktie.

Here's a personal story. In 1979 I applied for a Churchill Fellowship, in the faint hope of being able to study in the U.S. I was granted an interview. At the time I was twenty-six, idealistic, still very much a hippy, rebellious and socially awkward. Minutes before it was time to go to the interview, I suddenly thought about what to wear. I almost went in an open-necked shirt, then thought better of it. I borrowed a tie from a friend down the road, went to the interview and won the fellowship! I was lucky. It was a small town, and by chance several of the interview panel knew my work – but without the tie, I don't think I would have 'qualified'.

A tie symbolises something very profound – *a willingness to fit in or to submit*. Every day outside the law courts you will see people standing in suits and ties who look like they have never dressed that way before in their lives. No-one is fooled by this. Everyone – the suit-wearers, the judges – know that this is a requirement to 'look' like you are trying to be a respectable person. To do otherwise would be to invoke the wrath of the system. But the symbolism is clear. It says, 'See, I am willing to go through the motions. I will be a good boy'.

At work a tie says, 'I am willing to put up with this discomfort' and therefore 'I am willing to put up with other indignities and constraints to get and keep this job'. (Can

I polish your boots with my tie?) It's important to see a tie for what it is. It's a slave collar.

(Class is a funny thing. Many men have long discovered too late that rising in the class hierarchy does not make you freer – in fact, the reverse. If you are a blue-collar worker, the company wants your body but your soul is your own. A white-collar worker is supposed to hand over his spirit as well. There's a beautiful scene in the film, *The Fringe Dwellers*, where the Aboriginal men sit together making jokes about the poor white man spending his weekends mowing the lawn and washing the car.)

It's not just the tie – a whole uniform goes with it (interesting word, uniform). In the U.S. there is a slang term for the men who do the paperwork, attend to the boring details of the business world. These men are called 'suits'. The millionaire in *Pretty Woman* strikes a deal and leaves the details to 'the suits' to tidy up. Suits (and the men who wear them) are characterised by their lack of colour, their lack of individuality.

Ride the commuter planes between capital cities any morning at 7 a.m. or late in the evening and you will be amazed at the vast numbers of look-alike, grey-faced men, moving endlessly to and fro across the country in the dreadful lifestyle of the 'executive'. They might be flying First or Business class, they are first off the plane, into the Club Lounges, but no-one in their right mind would envy them. They are privileged eunuchs, leading a dry and joyless life.

THE DEMON

WHEN I AWOKE THIS MORNING
EXHAUSTED FROM MY REST
A DEMON DARK AND TERRIBLE
WAS SITTING ON MY CHEST.

HE PINNED ME TO THE MATTRESS
AND SEIZED ME BY THE HEAD
HE PRESSED HIS KNEES AGAINST MY HEART
AND OVERTURNED THE BED.

HE DRAGGED ME TO THE MIRROR
AND SHOWED ME MY DISGRACE
THEN TOOK A RAZOR IN HIS CLAW
AND DRAGGED IT DOWN MY FACE

SOME FADED RAGS HE BOUND AROUND
MY SHOULDERS AND MY HIPS
AND POURED A CUP OF STEAMING MUCK
BETWEEN MY FADED LIPS

AND THEN HE TOOK THOSE WILTED LIPS
AND IN HIS EVIL STYLE
HE PARALYSED THE CORNERS UP
INTO A PLEASANT SMILE

A MASTERPIECE IN WICKEDNESS
THIS LAST SADISTIC JOKE
HE SENDS ME OUT INTO THE WORLD
A SMILING SORT OF BLOKE.

Beware the mortgage trap

How does this all happen? How do intelligent men become so ensnared? After all, no-one forces us to compete in the rat race. Our system has one outstanding way of holding men in place – it's called a mortgage. A mortgage is a good idea gone wrong. It isn't the invention of bankers – the idea of owing for a lifetime has a long tradition. The feasters at a New Guinean wedding, for example, consume so many pigs and yams that a young man will spend his life repaying the debt. As depicted in the film *Witness*, Amish people will gather in their hundreds to build a large, beautiful barn in a single day, which will set up a newlywed couple for a lifetime of farming. The whole community will help and this young couple will in turn help out at many other barn-raisings in the course of their lifetime. This is a system of mutual support, with a mutual obligation, which has kept the Amish safe, prosperous, recession-proof and with low divorce rates for several centuries.

What *we* have is the mortgage system, which allows you to have a house, from the start of your adult life and to spend your life paying for it. Your obligation is not to people but to institutions. (Lose your job, fail to pay and faceless institutions will throw you out.) When you go for that vital interview at the bank (wearing your tie, of course!), you walk out with a hundred thousand dollars. It's a miracle! But something else happens, something they don't tell you about. *You leave a testicle behind!* The bank manager keeps it in a jar in his safe, along with all the others! If ever in your life you get the urge to do something risky, exciting, different or adventurous, chances are you will not because *you won't have the balls to do it!*

Somehow, to be a free man, you have to escape this trap. You could live in the country where houses cost less. You could stop competing with your neighbours and drive the oldest car in your street. You could give your children more of your time, instead of a private school education. You could take a year off and just think it all over!

Putting the heart back into work

It isn't the fact of working that does harm. Work is good – it's what men love to do. It's the nature of the work that is the problem. If you do a job that lacks heart, it will kill you. The strongest predictor of life expectancy in a man is whether he likes his job. Two elements – the lack of real purpose and the lack of personal control – are the main problems.

Our ancestors laughed as they worked and sang; they enjoyed the rush of the hunt, the steady teamwork of digging for yams or the discovery of a honey-filled tree. Watch any documentary or archival footage of preliterate people, you will see the same thing. Life was often hard but it was rarely without laughter. In time, though, cultures evolved away from the forest and the coast and into the village and the town. We did the work that others commanded, and it became a grind – increasingly repetitive. It was a numbing of human senses and a subjugation of ourselves beneath the need just to survive. Today, as we verge on the 21st century, work has become more comfortable but not more fulfilling. It's still a separate compartment in life – something you tolerate in exchange for 'real' living in the time left over from doing your job, getting to your job and recovering from your job! Work today drives an unhealthy wedge into the very core of our life. The time has come to heal it.

Most people today, men and women, do work they do not much like – jobs that are beneath them. When I was a teenager, there was an idea being introduced in schools called 'career guidance'. It's aim was to help you find something you liked to do. But underneath it all we dimly sensed the real purpose. Since you had to work to purchase the good life, the aim was just to find the best paying job you could *tolerate*. That's what jobs were. Why else would you do them? (At least in those days there was a choice – with unemployment rates today, to have any job is seen as a privilege and being choosy is a sin.)

We have to fight this selling-short of human potential – reject it in our own lives, and not pass it on to our kids, blighting their childhood with recessionary gloom. The purpose of adolescence is to find what you really love to do. Once you find this you must learn to do it well enough, so that it will pay as a by-product. You will either be happy, or rich *and* happy! The aim is to have work that your heart is in. Work that makes you jump out of bed in the morning, keen to get started. This is not so hard as you might have been led to believe.

The eight levels of fulfilling work

What follows are eight criteria for assessing your working life. If you achieve any one of these, you deserve to feel good. If you feel bored and stuck in your work, then look to the next stage as your guide. These are not for use in comparing self and others. They are measures of individual heroism. A brain-injured man learning to feed himself may show more courage than a great general.

1 Do you do your share?
This begins early. Even a three-year-old can and should contribute around the house. You can be an unemployed teenager, living at home, and still add to the wellbeing of your household. Perhaps you care for younger children, cook meals, fix up the house, grow food in a garden, take classes, travel and learn about the world, as money allows. You can feel proud that you contribute as well as receive. Remember it was business tycoons who caused Australia's recession. What we need is more people who can simply carry their own weight.

2 Can you support yourself?

If you have a job or earn an income of some kind then you are not drawing on the resources of the nation. They can be used to care for others who haven't that accomplishment. You are a plus to society. This is the second step on the way. If this is all you ever do, you are an asset.

3 Is your job one that allows you to improve the lives of others?

Many unglamorous jobs – bus drivers, shopkeepers or doctors' receptionists, for example – have an important daily impact on hundreds of people they deal with. By realising that your real work is the contact you make with people, and by doing so in a friendly, interested way (not just carrying out the mechanics of your task), you can have a positive effect on the people you deal with and the people they deal with in turn.

4 Are you a provider for others?

Even if you only have a job that is very routine, supporting others is an achievement. Partner, children and family can benefit and get a good start under the umbrella created by your being the provider. You support the continuation of life and the generations that follow.

5 Does your work provide an infrastructure for the work of others?

Does your job create other jobs, give leadership and structure, opportunity and growth to other people? Your work or business may provide a niche for others that otherwise might not have existed.

6 Do you train and develop other people, enhancing their lives and futures?

No-one is grown-up when they begin work. We all need mentors and father-figures in the workplace, not just bosses. We need men and women who have our interests at heart. Sit down and write out the qualities of the kind of boss you would like to work for. Then see if you can match up to these qualities. Being a mentor and friend can be the most satisfying aspect of any job.

7 Does your work help protect the earth, its people and its life?

Doctors have an ancient rule – at least, do no harm. If we all applied this in our jobs, it would be interesting. For instance, you may make a good living distributing a farm chemical which is banned in Europe yet protected in Australia by powerful lobbying. Doing this would not be illegal, but clearly (like the plumbers at Auschwitz, say) you are part of something fundamentally bad. Would a caring shopkeeper refuse to sell cigarettes – to anyone? A movie maker needs to ask – what kind of movies does the world need? The ad man – what kind of ads? A journalist – what kind of news items? A real man has to look at these questions. It isn't enough just to be successful. You have to ask – successful at what?

8 Does your work use your innate abilities and talents so that it is unique and powerful in its effect on the world?

Fred Hollows knew how to fix eyes and how to organise others to do the same – on a global scale. John Lennon knew how to write songs. Comedians like Glyn Nichols and Anthony Ackroyd know how to make people not just laugh but smile on the inside. Some men know how to solve crimes, others can heal pain, paint pictures, make violins, train dogs, ride a wave, kick a ball, lay cement, design glorious buildings, make new laws. We need them all.

You have things inside you to do. These lie dormant waiting to be expressed. How can you tell? You will know – an unexpressed urge will actually hurt you if it isn't let out. You have to set yourself free.

Same job, different attitude

Realistically, for many men, the trick is *finding the heart in the work you already do*. It is possible to be an honest real-estate salesman, lawyer, politician, doctor and so on. But such people are still the exception to the rule. Think about your job. How would you go about removing the facade that is traditionally built up in your line of work, so that you can be more of the real you? I have a friend who is an architect. He has given up the entire concept of deadlines, realising that the word itself is sinister. He tells his clients in advance that he uses 'alive-lines' – realistic but flexible schedules that can be negotiated as they proceed – and that the result will be a better building.

I've seen a bank manager place before all other priorities the considerate development of his staff's careers. I've seen a shop assistant, a young man of about twenty or so, so gentle and tender in his handling of a confused old lady, that it brought tears to my eyes. These people are different from the norm, and they transform the banal situation into magic. They have the confidence that comes from some inner sense of what matters.

I don't think all work can be converted in this way. Some basically negative jobs, like politics as it is currently practised, environmentally damaging work or dishonest work like some kinds of selling, breed a paranoia that twists in on itself, however much the man denies that he gives a damn. Like St Paul on the road to Damascus, there comes a time to say – I Quit.

We have a recession because there is no growth in the economy. Yet we live in a finite world that cannot sustain growth anyhow – so an economic boom would be a disaster too! When mainstream men abandon their urge to compete – and simply enjoy being and doing what is useful, as opposed to profitable – then we will have the kind of stable economy the world needs. Instead of more factories and office towers, we will build a spiritual, intellectual and social infrastructure that will make us healthy, secure and self-sufficient – qualities that even measured in dollar terms will be impressive.

Retirement – an insult and a waste

Recently I heard David Mowaljarlai, a Kimberley Aboriginal elder, speaking at a men's gathering near Lismore about the life-cycle of a man in traditional society. One of the older (white) men present asked whether an Aboriginal elder ever retired.

David smiled and described the ceremony his people would conduct each year, in which the leader of a clan would have to climb to the top of a pole placed in the ground, thus proving that he was still strong enough to lead. I thought at the time how subtle a device this was, since most people would assume that the old man would want to stay as leader. And yet an old man ready to relinquish this burden would actually have a choice whether he made it to the top of the pole or not. 'Damn (chuckle, chuckle) I guess I just can't make it this year!'

Retirement is a source of some pain and ambivalence among many men. Perhaps this was the questioner's thought too, as he asked 'What then ?'

David searched in his mind for the right word. 'I don't know what you call it in English. The old fella – be becomes no longer the leader, he's the "manual"'.

For a moment I thought he meant manual labour. I envisaged a disgraced elder cleaning up around the camp.

People looked blank. David tried to explain. 'You know, like the book you get with your car.' Someone caught on. 'Oh, the manual – the instruction book.' 'Yes,' said David, 'when the new leader, he comes across something he can't handle, he hasn't seen before, he goes and consults the "manual"'!

So beyond full-time leadership and all its worries lies a specialist place, honoured – because when the time comes, their knowledge will be needed. In Aboriginal tradition nothing is wasted, certainly not the life-preserving knowledge of the elderly.

In American factories and car plants, many older managers and foremen were fired in the Eighties as accountants and economic rationalism took over the way things were done, by the 'bottom line'. But things started to go wrong. More and more, according to *In Search of Excellence* author, Tom Peters, these old men were brought back, on high pay and short hours, to walk around the plant and oversee things. They had the sixth sense, the subtle knowledge, to tell when a machine was about to go out of phase, or an interpersonal problem was developing to crisis point. They could act before the problem *was* a problem, because they knew how to read the signs. There is no substitute, you see, for experience.

Retirement, for men, is a bad idea. When you retire, you die – although your body might go on for a few more years. The aim is to find a way to take your 'elderhood' onto the next phase. Now is the time you make your greatest contribution, however subtle.

Understanding the father-role of bosses

The Men's Movement gives great weight to leadership – what it calls Zeus energy. This is the ideal of leaders with no ambition other than the wellbeing of their community. At present, idealists don't see leadership as attractive or even a sound idea. And so the leadership roles are taken by power freaks and egotistically driven men – the people with the worst possible reasons for being in charge.

Symbols matter. The symbol of what it means to be a man is 'The King'. When my grandfather was born in industrial England, the king was George V. My grandfather, like tens of thousands of others, was named George and he also called his own son – my father – George. The importance of this cannot be overstated. Today we have boys called Wayne, Sean and Darrel. (From John Wayne, Sean Connery, etc.) Royalty, it seems, has let us down.

With one or two exceptions, Australia too has had disappointing leaders. Yet it's not impossible in the modern world to have a leader who is revered. When Sweden's Prime Minister, Olaf Palme, was gunned down as he walked home from the cinema with his wife one warm evening, the Swedish people wept openly in the streets. Revered was not too strong a word for this man. People told news crews, 'We needed him, the world needed him'. Palme had stood against apartheid and the Vietnam war and had worked for nuclear disarmament for over twenty years. He was the most natural and unassuming man you could meet – he could have been your next-door neighbour. He had presided over a country so nonviolent that his own death was one of only three handgun deaths in the whole of Sweden that year. (New York City alone has about twelve a night, four thousand a year.)

In Australia, our leaders and managers make the fatal mistake of thinking that leadership is all about economics. They misunderstand that people are led by the heart. True leadership means getting involved with people – it's an interpersonal job, a fathering job. To succeed as a leader you have to have been fathered well yourself and be able to bring this to a wider stage. As a nation we select people with the wrong motivation. True leaders have as their goal the wellbeing of their team and, beyond that, the wellbeing of the human species. They view themselves as servants.

It's instructive to watch video footage of leaders, the Dalai Lama, Gandhi, Churchill, Bob Brown, Nelson Mandela and Fred Hollows. Real leaders are like little boys, playful and emotionally available, yet when the need arises, they can muster fierce intelligence and purpose. They have good brains, but are driven by their hearts. Most leaders today are not even oriented in this way. Pompous and stiff, they see their teams as people to stand on, their consciousness is outwards and upwards – to 'furthering their own career' or 'covering their own tail'. A truly good leader is driven by one maxim, 'How can I help these people who have

placed their trust in me?' They are not egotistical – leadership is a cloak they put on, a job they do and which they
then step back from.

To be a leader, a man has to draw on basic fatherly
qualities – nurturing, praising, challenging, disciplining,
teasing, following the individual development of their staff.
A woman has to draw on motherly qualities, which are
different, yet not so different. This can be done intensely
on a personal basis with only a dozen or so people,
although one's availability must go wider. One needs to
understand the power of symbols to unite and inspire and
give purpose.

If this interest and care is not invested, followers will
react with as much hurt as if their own father were hurting
them – the symbolic link is that strong. The public service
in many parts of Australia has sustained damage from this
kind of mismanagement in recent times that will take
decades to restore.

The joy of the team

Billions of dollars are spent by organisations on studying
'Total Quality Management' (TQM), hanging off cliffs, practising management simulations, developing consultative
work groups and so on. In spite of these often quite
admirable programs, modern workgroups remain stunningly
mediocre. The leadership has not provided a purpose which
their people can actually believe in. Not just, 'We make the
best pies', but that we are doing something that has a larger
meaning. This can be a spiritual need as much as a practical
one. For instance, a football team achieves a kind of
spiritual glory when it unifies itself and overcomes the odds,
when everyone involved transcends themselves. In the film
Strictly Ballroom, the young man (played by Paul Mercurio)
achieved this for himself and his broken-down father, but
only through the support of his 'team'. It was the collective
effort, each person 'coming good' that made the last scenes

of this movie so glorious. What am I saying? That the world needs scientific progress, it needs environmental solutions, but equally it needs football and flamenco dancing!

Eventually in our work, we have to ask the big, 'So what?' The sales figures, the promotion – what do they mean? When we explain to our teenage kids why we have missed their school play, we need to have a good answer. As we sit in the Whispering Gums Retirement Home, waiting for the comfort of a cool bedpan, the question will come up, 'What was my life worth?'

Men yearn to believe in themselves and in something greater. If a leader can identify such a purpose and convey it to his team, then they will follow passionately. The larger purpose takes over their immediate self-interest and lends wings to their efforts. People under these conditions work wonders, they actually help each other, become creative, awaken in the early hours of the morning inspired. This was what happened when Lucas Aerospace shifted from making bombers to producing artificial limbs. It happened when retired U.S. Army engineers decided to go back to Vietnam to take out the mines left in the war. It happened when Fred Hollows formed groups to make artificial eye lenses in impoverished countries around the world. There are all kinds of examples of this in the world.

Men have worked in teams for so many millions of years that the template is in every cell of our bodies. (In fact our bodies are teams of cells.) The pattern of the hunting clan just needs to be reactivated. Today most men have become compulsive loners in their work, with superficial camaraderie but no real sharing. Think how much better we will feel as we begin to pull together for goals we believe in.

In a nutshell

1 Burn your tie or use it to tie up the tomato plants.

2 Either find a job you can believe in or find something to believe in about your job.

3 If you're a boss, realise that you are a father-figure. You are there to nourish and care for your people, so they can do their jobs. Give more positive feedback. Vary your expectations to suit individuals. Share your vision. Ask people their opinions. Confront irresponsibility. Don't put people down. Discipline in private, praise in public.

4 If you're in a team, realise that by dropping competition, you can achieve amazing goals, especially if they are goals you can believe in.

5 Love, fun and idealism have as much place at work as in any other aspect of life.

6 If you must retire, don't retire from life. Become an elder. Above all, stay involved.

Other voices

- The company, the church, the university, want a passive man.

Robert Bly

Don't Burn Your Tie
Walker Feinlein, Professor of Textile Anthropology at the University of Hobart, strongly counsels against burning your tie in a fit of masculinist fervour. Bra-burning in the Sixties was largely a media creation, he explained, arising out of an accident with a faulty cigarette lighter. Alternative uses for ties include using them to stake the tomato plants, throwing a couple in the car boot for use as an emergency fanbelt, or tying several ties together to create a colourful drum strap for those all-night sessions! Professor Feinlein predicted ties would soon go the the way of the frock coat and cummerbund. (Never heard of a cummerbund? I rest my case!) By the year 2000, ties will only be worn by elderly lesbians and spokesmen for the Wilderness Society!

Michael Leunig *(in an interview with Caroline Jones)*
Yes, I think ... men have become enslaved. Possibly it's the industrialisation process. They've become removed from Nature, which kept them connected to feelings. Zorba the Greek is not easily found amongst contemporary men. *(Laughs)* They seem to be enslaved and somewhat castrated, I think, and the fact that men have to get up in the morning and go off to work (this is how it was traditionally) ... I used to see my father do this: get up at 5.30 a.m., go off to a cold meatworks, come home late, exhausted, every day of his life. He just wasn't in the race; he didn't have a chance in many ways. He had to be tough; he wasn't allowed to have those feelings.

And I think this has suited women to some extent too, or a lot of women I mean, just as feminism seemed to women to be throwing off the role that was allotted to them, I think this has yet to happen to men. Men are carrying so much expectation and misunderstanding. It hasn't been easy to be a male through the feminist years because to be constantly told that all men are rapists and all men are exploitative, and all men are pigs, and blah blah blah, ... while one recognises the truth in part of that, it's not good, it doesn't help men at all, it's made men retreat. Men have lost their nerve a bit, as they need to, but I just hope it goes on and they rise up a bit against – not women, because they need to love women and to care for women, women aren't the enemy. Maybe it's a sort of capitalism, maybe it's consumerism; maybe it's all these things, that 'the system' as they say, has enslaved men. They've been made into a 'work unit', an economic unit, they have to keep earning all this money. (*Caroline adds*) *And keep this system going which, as you pointed out earlier, really isn't serving us terribly well, it would seem now, and that's heartbreaking ...*

It's a terrible thing ... If it was serving us well, if we had marvellous schools and it was all a bit more humanistic, and fulfilling, then, well, let's work hard. But all this hard work, and distress, and this debt – for what? So you can watch some cheap video, and eat junk food, and look at your neighbourhood falling apart, and the shopping centre full of plastic signs and noise and carelessness? Men need to, ... I think men often define themselves in some way or feel connected to this world by their skills, their dexterity, the way they can make things and do things. They're becoming more useless, it seems, more enslaved, more trapped. They sit at desks, and they've got to look good – they've got to look so damn good now, and so neat and pressed, and the hair's got to be just right, and they've got to smell nice and stare at a screen all day. The regimentation is appalling, and what does this do to the human spirit? What is it doing to the spirit of man? If there be an essential male psyche or something, I imagine it's having a terrible effect.

When do you get the fullest sense of being who you are?
I like being in the dirt a bit, getting my hands dirty, or
something like that. What about sex? I mean, why does no
one mention sex when they're asked what they most like to
do? That's an important thing I do. I like sex, I like eating, I
like going to bed at night – those fundamental things. These
are terribly central and important. I like gardening, I like digging a hole. I like to construct something, I like to paint. ...
I think those things are sacred, and they are common to us
all, I would think. Oh, and this other thing ... I think that
people are deprived somewhat by modern life; the chance to
be of some clear value to the society or to a person, to save
someone's life, or to pick someone off the road or to help
them. You watch people in a country town if there's a
bushfire. Everyone just leaps to get out and do a bit for each
other, and it brings out this lovely vitality, and people discover all levels within themselves.

- One man whom I know, saw one day, while meditating, a
  man of light at the end of a corridor, nine-feet tall with a
  spear. The man of light approached and said, 'If you don't
  make something of your life I will take it from you'. My
  friend was then thirty-eight years old.

  Robert Bly

- I am not a mechanism, an assembly of various sections.
  And it is not because the mechanism is working wrongly
  that I am ill.
  I am ill because of wounds to the soul, to the deep emotional self.
  And the wounds to the soul take a long, long time, only
  time can help.
  And patience, and a certain difficult repentance
  long, difficult repentance, realisation of life's
  mistake, and the freeing oneself

from the endless repetition of the mistake
which mankind at large has chosen to sanctify.

D.H. Lawrence

• I have chosen to emphasise what I think is believed to be
the most central source of men's alienation – the absence of
a sense of abiding meaning or, as I prefer to say, vocation,
in our lives.

Sam Keen

• ... forty-eight percent of American men are now employed
by one of the top-ten giant corporations, or by the US government.
... writers in eastern Europe (pre-*glasnost*), where a charac-
teristic state of bureaucracy has been in force for several
generations, write about the emotional stagnation, mingling
resentment, malice and shame that results from bureaucratic
control.

Robert Bly in *Wingspan*

• Without work, all life goes rotten. But when work is soul-
less, life stifles and dies.

Albert Camus

• What the father brings home today is usually a touchy
mood, springing from the powerlessness and despair, mingled with long-standing shame and the numbness peculiar
to those who hate their jobs. Fathers in earlier times could
often break through their own humanly inadequate tempera-
ments by teaching ropemaking, fishing, posthole digging, ...
animal care, even singing and storytelling. That teaching
sweetened the effect of temperament.
Even mean men are sweet when they teach.

Robert Bly

• At these gatherings ... I am reminded in a very deep way
that the Men's Movement is a part of Mother Earth, and that
saving her and her children, and loving the men and women

who want to love us, is what the Men's Movement is all about ...

John Lee in *At My Father's Wedding*

• Men who can prevent themselves from giving everything away to work and to the world find themselves able at last to enter the walled space, inside which certain magical events take place.

Robert Bly

• The men who attend groups and gatherings ... want to find a new image of masculinity and a new meaning for the word 'man'. They are ready to shed their old skins. They arrive at the gatherings thinking their sickness of mind, body and spirit forces them to face their demons. But really their courage has led them there. The truly 'sick' men are still not identifying their problems and will not come to men's groups, men's centers, men's gatherings or read books about men's wounds. Those men are still very likely projecting their problems onto women, children, other men and other nations. The men who come to heal are by and large the healthiest men on the planet. They are strong enough to admit their hurt and to say, 'I'm scared but I'm here. I will show up and face my pain.' And after a few hours in the company of other, supportive men, many will reveal their fears for, what is for some, the first time in their lives.

John Lee in *At My Father's Wedding*

10
Real Male Friends

Two farmers stand in the dusty yard of a property. One is a neighbour, come to say goodbye, the other is watching as the last of his furniture is packed onto a truck. The farm looks bare – stock gone, machinery sold. Two teenagers stand by the car, the wife sits inside it, eyes averted.

The two men have farmed alongside each other for thirty years, fought bushfires, driven through the night with injured children, eaten thousands of scones, drunk gallons of black tea and cared for each other's wives and kids as their own. They have shared good times and bad. Now, one is leaving, bankrupt. He will go to live in the city, where his wife will support them by cleaning motels.

'Well,' says the mate. 'I'll be off then.'

'Yeah,' says the other. 'Thanks for coming over.'

'Look us up sometime.'

'Yeah, I reckon.'

And they climb into their vehicles and leave. And while their wives will correspond for years to come, these men will never exchange words again.

So much unspoken. So much that would help the healing to take place from this terrible turn of events. What pain would flow out if one was to say, 'Listen, you've been the best mate a bloke could want' and looked the other straight in the eye as he said it. Or if they had spent a long evening together with their wives, full of 'remember whens' punctuated with tears and easing laughter. If, instead of standing stiff-armed and choked, they could have had a long strong hug, from which to draw strength and assurance, as they faced the hardship their futures would bring. The farmer leaving the land will not find the opportunity for any of these supports, comforts or appreciations. He will be a massive risk for suicide, alcoholism, cancer or accident, as he twists up inside to suppress the emotions his body feels.

Men, you see, don't have friends – at least not in those countries cursed with an Anglo-Saxon heritage. In Australia we have 'mates', with whom we share a straitjacket agreement on which subjects we never discuss! A subtle and elaborate code governs the humour, the put-downs, the ways in which serious feeling or vulnerability is deflected. All this is well known and often written about. So it's time to make a change.

Little boys start out warm and affectionate. You will see them in the younger grades of school, arms about each other. And at this age they still are tender and kind to younger children, unfussed about being with girls and able to cry over a dead pet or a sad story. So what goes wrong? Let's find out.

Proving you're a man

We've already said that men are absent from the lives of little boys. So are older boys – since in our society we isolate each age group and expect them to mix only with same-age, same-sex children. This is an odd arrangement, since little boys love to be around older boys in every village and slum and tribe around the world. By comparison, the world of the little boy in primary school is a harsh and scary one. Because there is no natural leadership from older children, the group is unskilled in cohesiveness and lacks real protection. It becomes the law of the jungle – the kind of conditions portrayed in *Lord of the Flies*. The result (worse in a single-sex school), is a very physical and intimidating pecking order.

Paul Whyte, of the Sydney Men's Network, uses an exercise to help women understand what it is like to be a boy in the schoolyard culture. He asks them to imagine that their membership of their gender depends on their being able to physically defend themselves against others of their gender. That is, imagine if being a woman meant having to fight, physically, with any woman who came along and having to hold your own. If you couldn't do this, you would be beaten and you would be accused of not being a woman! This is life for boys at school. Violence is an ever present threat, and proving yourself adequate, through physical strength, a continual issue. This portrayal certainly describes my childhood. How about yours?

Proving you're not gay

Boys feel a strong need to prove their 'masculinity'. Most parents will notice how their son drops his voice an octave when his friends are around – or refuses to kiss his baby sister goodnight if a mate is visiting.

Into this scheme of things, especially as puberty arrives, comes a strange twist. The existence of homosexuality as a biological fact in the human race, combined with many people's inability to simply be comfortable with this variation in type, means that the dread of being thought to be gay hangs over the head of any boy who is different in any way from the norm. The risk is great – and varies from being consequently rejected, ridiculed, beaten or even killed, depending on the severity of the culture. Our non-acceptance of gays actually exacts a severe price on every straight young man. It leads to the self-censoring of any kind of warmth, creativity, affection or emotionality amongst the whole male gender. 'If I'm not "macho", then I might be seen to be gay.' (In the movie *Mr Mom*, the man stayed home for a time to mind his children. He wore a hard hat all day and kept a chainsaw ticking over by the door just in case a man dropped in!)

When we oppress gay people, we oppress ourselves as well. No-one feels free to be himself or herself.

The scourge of competition

Competitiveness – as a personality trait – stems from compulsively searching for approval that never comes. Even winning – as many top athletes find – is not enough. Yet given adequate approval from their mentors, boys and men do not have this compulsion to impress – they settle down to learning for its own sake, less concerned with being biggest and best. Glorious diversity, such as in Balinese art and culture, replaces obsessive greed and acquisitiveness.

> Everyone agreed that condoms were a great idea except for one thing – while men came in different sizes, condoms only came in one standard size. Manufacturers had cottoned-on early that no self-respecting man would walk into a chemist shop and ask for a six pack of *small* condoms!
>
> The conversation turned quiet at this point as each person made their own inner reflections. Finally someone hit on an answer. The smallest size could be called 'large'! What about the larger sizes? The atmosphere became ribald at this stage. It was finally agreed after many alternatives that there should be three sizes of condom – 'large', 'huge' and 'oh my God!'
>
> Adapted from a story in the *Whole Earth Review*

Competition is the bane of men's lives. To this day, when I sit down in a public place, beside a swimming pool, for example, I relax and feel good if there is no-one else around. If another man arrives, I first run a check that he is no physical threat – that he is not about to mug me. No-one has ever mugged me or hurt me since childhood, but the feeling still lives. (Women understand this reflex, for different reasons.) Then I get to assessing whether he is stronger, has better clothes or is more athletic. If he is with a woman, I look for signs that she doesn't really like him! If the car park is within view, I check out his car for comparison with my own – a good guide to income and status, as well as taste. Even if he is friendly and a conversation starts, I consider in what light to present myself. The inner competition goes on and on – I seem caught in a basically hostile and insecure obsession with comparisons.

I am now retraining myself through Men's Movement ethics to change this useless pattern. I am teaching myself to see other men as brothers, with good things to give and to receive. I have always felt this way about women, but why not men too? This is leading to a huge change in attitude and a huge boost in my enjoyment of half the human race.

> Males who are denied appropriate physical affection with other males while growing up become people who never mature. In fact many men who are so denied will strongly repress their need for manly affection. You can see these men in any football game or boxing match. They seem to thrive on the violent aspects of male contact, while distancing themselves from any form of intimacy.
>
> When men are allowed to freely experience the love and support of other men, they begin to question competition in our society. This questioning engenders a willingness to engage in more service-oriented projects and activities whose aim is to nurture and protect the planet.
>
> Here lies the power of the New Masculine Soul. It all begins with an embrace.
>
> Barry Cooney in *Wingspan*

Beyond competition

The Xervante people of Brazil divide manhood up into eight stages of growth. These peer groups stay very close throughout life, and they are also helped by those in the group higher up in the sequence. Each year the Xervante hold running races for each age group in turn. These races look like a contest but they are not. When a runner falters or trips, the others pick him up and run with him. The group always finishes in a pack.

In fact it's not a race at all in the sense we mean it – though everyone puts in a huge effort. It's a celebration of manhood – an expression of surplus vitality. This is a culture that has survived thousands of years by cooperation. They don't have to prove they are men, they celebrate that they are men. Marvin Allen says it beautifully – 'I defy anyone, anywhere in the world, to "prove" that they're a man'. In fact it's a ridiculous concept. Women wouldn't entertain the concept of 'proving' they're women.

Friends offer enormous comfort. They help to structure your time. They show you that you belong and can be cared about. Perhaps this is why men traditionally cook at barbecues. It's a declaration that 'men can feed you too'. If you don't believe this, listen to the banter which takes place between men and women over the quality of the sausages and chops!

A man who lacks a network of friends is seriously impaired from living his life.

Friends alleviate the neurotic overdependence on a wife or girlfriend for every emotional need. If a man, going through a 'rough patch', gets help from his friends as well as his partner, then the burden is shared. If his problems are **with** his partner (as they often are) then his friends can help him through, talk sense into him, stop him acting stupidly and help him to release his grief.

A male-out – men supporting men in crisis

Two years ago, in a large public service department in Hobart, a man in his forties was given a retrenchment notice. He had been a dedicated, professional worker and his boss did not have the guts to tell him personally. Instead, out of the blue, this man and a dozen others received a Roneoed letter in their mail box.

The man became irrational and, on the following day, purchased a gun, shredded work documents and greatly alarmed his wife and young children.

Several friends conferred about what to do. They settled on a course of action. They went to his house, taking food and sleeping bags, and spent the weekend living there, while his wife and children were sent elsewhere. They rostered themselves so that someone was always awake and with the man – who was too agitated to sleep very much. By the Sunday afternoon, after much talking, crying and holding, the man thanked his friends for stopping him from 'making an idiot' of himself and began to make concrete plans for his future. The friends stayed in touch and checked that things were in fact going well. His family came back home a few days later, and his life has progressed well.

The friends knew somehow that this was their job – it was a man's issue. Male friends can do these things where wives and other women probably cannot. Other men know how you are feeling. Men have issues – about being a provider for instance – which do not have a female equivalent. Only other men can help you learn about the ongoing process of being a man.

Communicating feelings

Millions of women complain about their husband's **lack** of feeling, his woodenness. Men themselves often feel numb and confused about what they really want. This is usually attributed to an irreconcilable split between men and women – the so-called 'battle of the sexes'. But what if men's inarticulateness simply comes from a lack of sharing opportunities (as opposed to bullshit sessions) ***with other***

men? If men talked to each other more, perhaps they'd
understand themselves better. Perhaps they would then
have more to say to their wives. It seems entirely possible
that only in the company of other men can they begin to
activate their hearts. Michael Meade says that just as men's
voices have a different tone, so do their feelings. We have
more than enough feelings, but they are not the same as
women's feelings. Once activated, we have no trouble
expressing ourselves.

The dehumanising of men

How many of you here are tall, rich, you know, successful,
powerful, got an eight-inch dong, got hair on your chest,
slender, muscular, always in control ... has anybody ...
we've got one over here! Only man here!!

There's a new definition of a man here, and it has at
least – ***at least*** – as much emphasis on loving and nurturing, as on providing and protecting.

Marvin Allen, addressing an audience of men

Men get set up in a serious double bind by the larger
society. They are asked – especially of late – to be more
intimate and more sensitive. However, they are still coached
in the possibility of being sent to war, still expected to be
tough when needed – because toughness *is* needed in this
life. We don't actually want men who are weaker – just
men who can shift gears when needed – which is a
considerable skill.

I have been married twice, and had several other relationships that ended badly. Like most women I have always
'listened' to men, but until today I never heard them. I
have never heard men talk to other men with such depth
and love. And I never imagined what it was like for men to
live with the knowledge that they must be prepared to kill,
or with the actual horror of battle. This weekend I feel like

I have been in a room with giants. I thank you for letting
me listen.

A woman observer in a Man's weekend

One writer described arriving with four friends seconds after
at a serious traffic accident. They stopped traffic, pulled
people out of vehicles, staunched serious bleeding and
comforted the family of two people who had been killed
outright. Three hours had passed before it was all over.

'What I would like to have seen', the writer said later,'
was a newspaper headline reading – "Five men control their
feelings in order to save lives in freeway carnage."' He was
pointing out that controlling one's feelings is a very valuable
part of male make-up. It has great survival value, and all
women, deep down, count on it. Being able to also let go
of those feelings, when the time is right, is another matter
entirely.

At a gathering of men

A group of men sit in an afternoon seminar, a part of a
larger conference on the family. Women have been asked
not to attend this meeting. The atmosphere in the room is
different to the other seminars of the day – slightly sombre,
a little charged. A middle-aged woman who is lost puts her
head in the door, immediately senses the atmosphere,
mumbles an apology and disappears.

It's my job to lead this seminar. I sit quietly, getting
comfortable with the room, settling down into my body. I
have started thousands of seminars and talks, and know not
to disperse my own energy trying too hard to be 'friendly'.

When the time comes, I begin to speak and the group
slowly warms up. Unlike the vitality and the slight sense
of indignation you will find at a Women's Movement
meeting, in a men's group there is great reserve, even fear.
This is lightened a little by banter and warmth from some
of the older, more self-reliant men. As a forty-year-old man,

I stand midway – no longer brash or superficially confident, nor too much in love with the sound of my own voice. I have experienced enough loss and shame. I've learned respect for pain and endurance – which only makes me more respectful of those who have gone further. So I speak first to the older men and thank them for coming. I acknowledge explicitly that they have lived longer and deeper than I have. I ask for their help if I stray due to inexperience. Then we begin.

The discussion follows a kind of natural gravitational pull which, at this time in men's history, seems to be the way forward. We talk first about what is **not** working – rifts with fathers, painful experiences in marriage, parenthood, health. The invitation is for men to tell parts of their experience and simply listen to each other. One after another, men speak. As they speak, quietly and simply, eyes fill up and men begin to cry.

From time to time we break into smaller clusters of men, then return to share conclusions. It is hard to stop people talking. At the end, no-one wants to leave. It is another hour after the appointed time before the last man shares a long hug with me and goes on his way.

There is a pressure inside men which has been building up for a very long time. It's nothing complicated – just, 'How is your life going?' Yet this kind of conversation does not happen at the pub or the sporting club, or the Rotary or Church meeting. So the opportunity for a very natural and necessary part of men's soul development is missing from our lives. Imagine how tense women would become if they could never talk to other women. Understanding this, perhaps men's tension and numbness makes more sense. We've held back from each other for so long.

Grief

Grief expert Mal McKissock has said that when Australian men shut down their feelings, it starts to kill them. A bereaved man is eight times more likely to die in the two-year period following bereavement than a man with family intact. If a child in a family dies – a cot death, for instance – there is *a seventy percent likelihood that the parents' marriage will not survive the loss*. We simply – and urgently – must provide a means for men to express their grief. McKissock explains that failing to grieve leads to a loss of passion in the whole of life. No-one wants to stay married to a block of wood, and so marriage disintegrates. Wives and partners have their own pain, and so often cannot provide what is needed. Mal McKissock believes that failing to feel one single emotion (in this case, sadness) leads to a shutdown in the full spectrum of feelings – anger, fear and warmth and love. This passion is what most of us men have lost and this is also what we stand to gain.

Crying is a simple physical act. When we cry our body produces its own healing chemicals which wash through our brain, healing the losses we've sustained. Once we've wept we can breathe freely, see clearly, feel the love of others and face the world again.

The better a man takes care of himself during these dark times, the sooner he passes through the dark night. The more damage and denial he does to himself, the longer he will take to heal, and the deeper will be the mistakes he makes along the way. More hearts will be broken in his attempts to heal his broken heart.

When a man grieves, he walks through 'the valley of the shadow of death', but he doesn't have to do this alone. When he comes out on the other side, he'll be lighter, less intense, less addicted, ready to love and be loved. If a lover comes near, he'll be ready for intimacy, and if she doesn't, he'll still be alright because he can now take care of him- self. He has a support group of people in his life whom hopefully he'll keep and nurture, and be nurtured by even with a new love.

Robert Bly in *To Be a Man*

A friend of mine lost his father at the age of eight. His
mother suicided two years later. He and his younger brothers were split up and sent to various relatives and rarely
saw each other until adulthood. When I met him, he was
a highly successful businessman, but troubled by sudden
rages which had lost him a number of employees. He had
two failed marriages and was just holding on in a third. By
now he knew that the problem was in him, and was ready
to talk. All he really needed to do was tell the story and
express the grief that went with it. A simple, profound act
which he had never done, with anyone, since childhood.
As he told his story, softly and slowly, he would suddenly
be overcome with great washes of tears and sobbing. Then
he would quietly go on. Gradually the most extraordinary
feeling of peace came into the room where we were sitting.
It's an experience I will never forget.

Fun and friendship

The other reason for male friends is to have fun. The kind
of fun that is noisy, energetic, affectionate, ribald, accepting, careful under the playfulness but free from
respectability or restraint.

> We called ourselves SPERM (the Society for the Protection
> and Encouragement of Righteous Manhood).'
>
> Sam Keen

> The harshness and zaniness of male companionship.
>
> Robert Bly

Some teenage boys near where I live did an unusual thing
– they had enjoyed some camping trips on the banks of the
Huon River, and decided they wanted to build a wooden
boat and sail down the river. Since they were young men,
rather than children, their parents gave the project their
blessing. With the help of one of the fathers, they found a

shed to work in, scrounged materials, worked weekends, saved money and the boat gradually took shape.

Things did not always go smoothly between them. One young man often failed to match the monetary contribution of the others, and added to the insult by borrowing money from them for other purposes. Since several of them had taken part-time jobs to raise funds, they were angry after a time and decided to confront him:

'You aren't pulling your weight. You're using us!'

Because of the bond that already existed between them, and the firm but unaggressive way they tackled him, he did not storm off. He thought it over, got a job and paid back what he owed. Character gets built in this way.

Another of the young boatbuilders had trouble with over-bearing parents with high expectations. The others noted his growing depression and consulted their parents about how to help. They decided to simply tell their mate up front.

'Listen, sport, you only have to live with your parents for another year. Hang in and get your HSC. Then your life's your own. You do what *you* want to do with your life. You can always live here in the boatshed!'

Islands of seriousness in a sea of good times. Everyone's lives are eased, stabilised and supported by these friendships. If you like a good read, Maeve Binchy's novels portray beautifully what friendship can do for young people.

Why shouldn't all men – young and old – have such a safety net in their lives? It could avoid all kinds of disasters.

In a nutshell

1 Weed out any kind of competition from your friendships, beyond the playful kind that makes sport more exciting.

2 Stop trying to prove you're a man. Just be one.

3 Be affectionate. Give straight compliments from time to time.

4 Listen to your friends' problems without trying to minimise them or give advice.

5 Join a men's group where men talk about their real lives and discuss painful topics as well as cheerful ones.

6 Don't be afraid of grief or tears. You probably have a backlog already.

7 Have fun with other men. Be noisy, wild and safe. Be proud of being male. Maintain a good network of friends.

11
The Wild Spirit of Man

In this chapter, we will look at three of the deepest aspects of the Men's Movement: initiation, the Wild Man and the Time of Ashes. These are the profound processes which turn boys into men. They help men to acquire the power that comes from being tuned in to the forces of life. They give a man the wisdom he will need to one day become an elder.

> For this is the journey that men make. To find themselves.
> If they fail in this, it doesn't matter what else they find.
> James A. Michener in *The Fires of Spring*

Religion, spirit and man

Throughout history, all the peoples of the earth have practised some kind of religion. It has always been a central force in their lives. The caves of Lascaux with their beautiful animal paintings are our earliest records of masculine ritual. In Aboriginal society, religious and associated cultural practices took up seventy percent of the time of the mature men. Even today, in spite of the divisions and bigotries that religion can foster, the forces of good – from social welfare

to world peace – have a strong religious component. And
the most potent and effective men and women – from
Nelson Mandela to the Dalai Lama – are those with religious
underpinnings to their life.

Why does religion matter? Often we feel lost and confused, and cannot figure our lives out. You cannot think
your way out of such a space, not always. At other times
there is a feeling that is elusive but unmistakable – that
life is beautiful, and that you are in the flow of things.
Ordinary ups and downs, pains and pleasures don't matter
when you feel you are on the right track. 'Spirituality'
simply means the direct experience of something special in
life and living. Religion, by which we mean organised group
activity and ritual, is an attempt to hold on to that feeling
and make it last. It is a container, which sometimes can
capture the quicksilver of real spiritual experience and
sometimes cannot.

People today have lost touch with the possibilities of
ritual – they think it has no use. Yet even when we use
the term 'empty ritual' we unwittingly acknowledge that
ritual can also be 'full'. Group efforts, such as ceremonies
and gatherings, are important ways to help each other stay
focussed on what matters, put a spiritual depth into our
lives and pull our perspective back to the big picture and
away from trivial concerns.

For a man today the brand of religion one chooses to
pursue is not so important. The differences between religions are only differences of style and technique. (The true
Christian, Buddhist and Aboriginal elder would find much
to agree about and explore together.) In a sense, any
spiritual path will do. To **not have** some kind of spiritual
practice in one's life, however, is a serious mistake.

We seek the connection beyond words with the holy masculine, the ineffable, the unspeakable. It is through giving
into that deep desire that we feel our grief, our joy and our
anger. The longing for connection can take us out of our

personal dramas and into our deepest feelings. Then we feel
alive and human, full of rich emotional experience.

George Taylor in *Wingspan*

I have treated many hundreds of patients. Among those in
the second half of life – that is to say over thirty-five –
there has not been one whose problem, in the last resort,
was not that of finding a religious outlook on life.

C.J. Jung

Have the old religions let us down?

The great traditional religions of the world have much that
is liberating and life-enhancing, but their image has become
enfeebled in the modern world. Christianity – ideally a
powerful and revolutionary force in society – is today most
visible in TV commercials for chocolate biscuits and frozen
dinners. The image most people recognise is of neutered
vicars and doddery old ladies having afternoon tea. Even the
Church's own advertising portrays it as wacky and offbeat.
For many adherents, too, religion has become just a habit –
merely a familiar social network. The beliefs and rituals for
many have lost their power and continue only as husks.

Falling between the decline of the old ways and the lack
of a new 'living' religion, the majority of men just believe
in nothing. As a result, they are ill-equipped to answer or
handle any of life's deeper questions. Modern man, for all
his bravado, is very frail in the face of difficulties. Suicide,
cynicism, greed, addiction, wait close beside this path. What
Fred Hollows called 'secular goodness' sounds good, but
doesn't quite do the trick. (After all, Fred himself was
deeply into poetry, which is another kind of mysticism.)

Some people wonder if the Men's Movement itself will
become a religion. I suspect, though, that like feminism it
will transform and revitalise existing religions. Certainly, for
many men, it is already putting a meaning into their lives
and providing a sense of brotherhood that they have never
experienced before. It will turn more men on to spiritual

and ritual concerns than anything else has done for hundreds of years.

A poet's job is not to save the soul of a man, but to make it worth saving.

James E. Fletcher

Family isn't a substitute

Many men, if questioned, locate the purpose for their lives, not in a spiritual path, but in pursuing the wellbeing of their family. They live for their family. Altruistic as it may sound, to make one's family all-important is spiritually parasitic. Living through your wife is very bad for you both. Making your children your purpose for living puts an unbearable burden on them. (One manifestation of this is the insane logic of the man who murders his wife and children and kills himself, to keep his family together! In their hearts men are life-preserving, and hence such occasions are thankfully rare.) It's quite appropriate and healthy to dedicate several decades of your life to meeting your family's needs, and enjoying the rewards of this. However it is very easy to lose a sense of self at the same time, and so create all kinds of problems.

In *Fire in the Belly*, Sam Keen tells of being helped by an older man-friend while going through a painful divorce. This man told him, 'There are two questions a man must ask himself: The first is, "Where am I going?" The second is, "Who will go with me?" If you ever get these questions in the wrong order you are in trouble!' Many men get the order wrong.

Learning from the past

'Where am I going?' is the critical question. 'Where have I come from?' might hold some of the answers. We **know** where we have come from: there is a trail running back behind you through the centuries, all the way to a

Cro-Magnon hunter half a million years ago. You are alive and here today because he was wise, tough, skilful, nurturing, courageous and able to work with the forces of the universe. You have the same superb capacities that he did. The problem is to retrieve the software. Only then can you move forwards.

The Men's Movement already has an image (some say an image problem!) of harking back to idealised older times, of primitive tribal gimmicks and rituals. While this can create some awkwardness and leave us open to ridicule, it isn't bad to look backwards. We could do with more of it – we need to borrow from our ancestors if we are to avoid being the generation that let the fires of survival go out! Ancient man was an environmentalist who knew how to thrive in the natural world in a sustainable way. Since the environment is now the biggest concern we have we clearly need all the help we can get! To overcome **personal** extinction too, men are looking for help. The Men's Movement is very interested in the bonding rituals, the symbols, the initiation rites and the guiding metaphors from ancient times. We are scavenging for tools that we can use to make the future.

Ecology as a spiritual path

We have already said (in the chapter on work) that your ultimate job as a man is to preserve life. We can add here that this work can only be done well using a spiritual source of energy and direction. Living a life that makes ecological sense isn't just a technical challenge but involves an inner change of orientation too. The biologist who goes out to study the rainforest from an objective point of view comes back changed by the experience. The nights under the massive forest canopy and the days peering into nature's mysteries have captured his soul. He changes from a dried-up 'nerd' to a passionate and newly balanced man.

There's every indication that ecology is becoming a new religion. It's equally possible, though, that the needs of our time will simply transform our existing religions to something more vibrant and purposeful, by turning more to nature and wildness and less to dogma and intellectual head-tripping. There are already emerging ecologically-aware forms of Christianity and Islam, Hinduism, etc. (Buddhism is already a superbly ecological religion.)

Many people are attracted to a more natural life, not just from 'save the earth' pragmatism, but because they are pulled to it by the wildness in their own nature. Indeed there are many who would claim not to be religious at all, yet the wilderness and the ocean are already their spiritual homes. The thirst for wildness is with us every day. (Hence *Jurassic Park* and the Japanese mania for koalas. Hence the barbecue, the beach and the national park!) It's natural to love nature. The more artificial life gets, the more people strive to redress the balance. Nature always offers the happiest way for humans. The closer modern man gets to inner and outer wildness, the better things will go.

This takes more than just sitting in a forest being groovy! Ancient cultures knew that to 'arrive' as a man in harmony with the outer world requires a long journey. It's an involved process requiring effort and care from parents and elders, lasting many years.

> We need to build a body, not on the parallel bars, but an activated, emotional body strong enough to contain our own superfluous desires (our higher yearnings). This wild man can only come to full life inside when the man has gone through the serious disciplines suggested ... .
>
> Robert Bly

Initiation – the breakthrough to manhood

Today you become a man on the day you turn eighteen. The results of this are clear to see – boys in men's bodies, everywhere you look. In centuries gone by, becoming a man was a long, planned process. It required ritual and effort – and the deliberate, active intervention of older men. This ritual and effort, although very diverse in its forms around the planet, was universally practised in every society – from Eskimo to Urdu – by every race and every time. It was the first thing that anthropologists noticed when they visited cultures other than their own. It had a name. It was called 'initiation'.

Here is a Kikuyu (East African) traditional initiation, described by Bly:

> The young men are taken away to a special place, they fast for three days, the older men then come to them and join in a circle – cutting their own veins to fill a bowl with blood from which the boys can take nourishment. In this ritual the boy learns a number of things. He learns that nourishment does not come only from his mother, but also from men. And he learns that the knife can be used for many purposes besides wounding others. Can he have any doubt now that he is welcome among the other males?
>
> Once that welcoming has been done, the older men teach him the myths, stories and songs that embody distinctively male values; I mean not competitive values only, but spiritual values. Once these moistening myths are learned, the myths themselves lead the young male far beyond his personal father and into the moistness of the swampy fathers who stretch back century after century.

Initiatory journeys you might have made

While these traditions are lost to us, we may have unwittingly found substitutes or equivalents which can yet be made to work. It may be necessary to breathe life into whatever relic traditions we have, and apply some common sense, to make a new rite of passage for ourselves and our sons.

Sometimes we stumble onto it unconsciously. One night, while reading the work of Joseph Campbell, the renowned mythologist, I realised that I had made at least one of these journeys myself. I'm sure many men will recognise the pattern from their own youth. According to Campbell, the initiatory journey always has three steps:

1 A separation from home and family and all that is familiar.

2 A frightening, difficult, but exhilarating journey, helped along by unexpected hospitality from strangers and help from mystical allies. So you face your vulnerability and break out of many youthful fears and neuroses.

3 Finally, a return home: the traveller apparently the same person, but forever changed.

When I was seventeen, I saw a poster inviting young Australians to go alone and live in a New Guinea village and experience 'stone age' life. The scheme was organised by a student group wanting to bridge gaps between Papua-New Guinean culture and the West. I joined up and went. With a New Guinean host, I lived on the coast of West New Britain, with people who still wore leaf clothes, lived in grass houses and told creation stories around the fires at night-time. It was scary and I was often way out of my depth, but it was also a beautiful time. On the journey home, ill and still culture-shocked, I stayed at a coastal airstrip with a young Australian man called Marcus, who was a patrol officer. He was an 'older' man of about thirty-five!

Though I didn't know it at the time, Marcus was one of the people on that trip who represented the 'helper' or 'mentor' of the initiatory journey. While I waited for the floodwaters to recede from the airstrip and a plane to take me home, I filled in the time talking with him about life. We sat each night looking out at the Bismarck Sea, listening to the waves on the black beach sand and the deep-voiced chanting from fishermen in passing canoes.

One night he told me about his own childhood – on a farm near Wilsons Promontory in Victoria. How one hot afternoon, his father had received a telegram informing him that his own father had died. Marcus watched while his father ate tea quietly and then set off into the bush at dusk. Marcus, still just a little boy, followed him at a distance, mesmerised.

He found his father sitting on a hilltop, overlooking Corner Inlet, with a harmonica, playing a long and mournful dirge. He had never heard his father play this instrument before. After listening for a time and fearful of being discovered, he left and snuck back home.

In Port Moresby, on the way home, I realised I had no gifts to bring my parents or myself and so I sold my air ticket on the Brisbane-Melbourne leg, to raise funds. Then I bought some artefacts and hitchhiked the last sixteen hundred kilometres home (an adventure in itself)! A week later, at about 2 a.m., I found myself at a highway phone-booth on a deserted road about thirty kilometres from home. I experienced a curious impulse – to not go home at all, but just keep travelling. I solved it uniquely. My tired, hungry, dirty self phoned home, to be rescued by my long-suffering parents! But my inner self has been travelling ever since. Like many of my generation, I'm still on the road.

I'm sure you too have made such journeys. The memory is so ancient and the idea so much part of human development, that we may carry it out in part without realising it. The magic still works.

In older times, these journeys were properly organised. People knew what they were doing. The Native American young men would sit motionless on a mountain top seeking their vision dream. But you can be sure stealthy watchers guarded them from pumas and other dangers. The young people of the old cultures were too loved and too valuable an investment to be hazarded needlessly.

A friend of mine, who teaches abseiling to young offenders and business executives, explained to me that in this apparently dangerous activity the safety is total. It isn't through pointless danger that we grow, but through the utmost care and trust in each other.

What are the elements of a good initiation?

First there is a clean break with the parents, after which the boy goes to the forest, desert or wilderness. The second is a wound that the older men give the boy, which could be a scarring of the skin, a cut with a knife, a brushing with nettles, a tooth knocked out. But we mustn't leap to the assumption that the injuries are given sadistically. Initiators in most cultures make sure that the injuries they give do not lead to meaningless pain, but reverberate out of a rich centre of meaning.

Where a man's wound is, that is where his genius will be.

Mircea Eliade

The old initiators took the boys into the forest or the desert, to give them a great prize – to teach them that they themselves were sacred beings. That's what initiation means. There was fear involved, and symbolic wounding, but this was done with great care and for important reasons. It was never meant to be sadistic. The masks, dancing, rituals, magical teaching and adoption of totems gave the young man a strong sense of belonging and honour. Initiation is a welcoming into a masculine spirituality, constructed in a way that ensures it will never be forgotten.

A Christian missionary in Uganda in the 1970s observed that certain of the young men in his college were thin and unhealthy, they lacked confidence, did not take wives and lived very poorly. He discovered that these were the ones who through circumstance – illness or travel – had missed out on initiation. They just never made it in life.

The attention young men received at initiation was simply an intensification of the continuous involvement that uncles, grandfathers, cousins and older siblings took with boys and young men to convey to them living skills, and male spirit and ways of doing things. None of these cultures would dream of leaving masculine development to chance in the way that we do.

Michael Ventura, in a magnificent essay called, 'The Age of Endarkenment', speaks of adolescent wildness and its challenge to our lack of ideas. Their music, their fashions, their words, their codes, he says, announce that the initiatory moment has come.

Those extravagances are a request for a response. Ventura remarks:

> Tribal people everywhere greeted the onset of puberty, especially in males, with elaborate and excruciating initiations – a practice that wouldn't have been necessary unless their young were as extreme as ours ... The tribal adults didn't run from this moment in their children as we do; they celebrated it. They would assault their adolescents with, quite literally, holy terror; rituals that had been kept secret from the young until that moment ... rituals that focussed upon the young all the light and darkness of the tribe's collective psyche, all its sense of mystery, all its questions and all the stories told to both harbor and answer those questions ... The crucial word here is focus. The adults had something to teach, stories, skills, magic, dances, visions, rituals. In fact, if these things were not learned well and completely, the tribe could not survive ... Tribal cultures satisfied the craving while supplying the need, and we call that initiation. This practice was so effective that usually by the age of fifteen a tribal youth was able to take his or her place as a fully responsible adult.
>
> Michael Ventura, quoted in *Iron John*

> A caution. Each of us has to know a great deal more about initiation than we do before we can meet this initiatory demand. But it wouldn't hurt to think.
>
> Robert Bly

Sport is one of the arenas in which we could, with minor changes, still make boys into men. Our family has a Christmas tradition (like thousands of other Aussie families) of the afternoon cricket match. Little boys glow with pride, basking in the praise of uncles and grandfathers. Little girls play, too, but it isn't so serious to them. The men perform, too, and enjoy the teasing of the women. Fathers bawl out their young sons for being too fussy about the rules – not giving the little ones a bit of leeway. The odd tantrum or sulk is sorted out with dad behind the barbecue. It's pure character-training, along with much celebration of just being men together, glad to be alive in a human body in the warm sunshine.

There is more involved than just 'hanging out' with the older men. The best of the culture has to be transmitted deliberately by the old men to the young. In the first chapter I described the suicide of a high school student. This boy was a friend of mine. There may well have been family or personal reasons behind his decision to end his life – I couldn't say. These weren't the kind of things boys talked to other boys about back then. He was obsessed with science. Science was his religion. Yet the values of science – especially physics which was his passion – are mechanical and empty. According to physics we are all just atoms spinning meaninglessly in infinity. Nothing matters. This was the best that our culture could give him. It grieves and angers me that all around us stood the riches of four thousand years of human culture and beauty, but this was not the curriculum of high school circa 1965. My friend got science for a religion, and it wasn't enough to keep him alive.

Designing a modern initiation

We find ourselves here in the age of computers and jet travel with a serious problem – how to create meaningful processes for turning our boys (and ourselves for that matter) into men.

There are many threshold events in the lives of young people which have aspects of initiation, and could, if we chose, be made more special and helpful to giving them a good start. For boys, owning a car, and/or getting a licence, is a significant step. (Perhaps the real reason young men steal cars is to steal manhood – since no-one cares a damn about helping them find their way to it legitimately.)

Think for a moment what a driver's licence means. Total mobility and participation in the adult world are suddenly possible. A car brings independence and a great boost in the girlfriend stakes! One is also suddenly able to endanger one's own and other people's lives – so there's a massive jump in responsibility, too. A young person having made this step would benefit from an adult dinner with one's parents and older relatives and friends to imbue the moment with both congratulation and gravity.

Other thresholds include the first job; the first date. The HSC exams are a major and important mark of maturity (perhaps too important). They, too, merit celebration and support. Puberty markers – like a bar mitzvah – call out for creative celebration and adult support.

Having one's own flat, surviving away from Mum's apron strings, feeding oneself and paying the rent are important things to experience. Young men who go from mum to wife without a self-sufficient phase between always strike me as lacking a certain something, like the uninitiated Ugandan men mentioned earlier.

The wound

There is an ingredient of initiation, especially emphasised by the Men's Movement (and in particular by that wing of the Movement linked to the Recovery movement and twelve-step programs, etc.) This is the concept of *the wound*. The wound has multiple meanings. It refers both to actual injuries of body and soul (which almost all boys sustain through normal life) and to ritual injury – used to cleanse all preceding injuries and make them heroic instead of tragic.

In attempting to explain why initiation in so many parts of the world involves physical pain, Bly reminds us of the inner process which teenage boys are inflicting on ***themselves***:

> Early adolescence is the time traditionally chosen for initiation to begin and we all recall how many injuries we received at that age. Adolescence is the time of risk for boys and that risk-taking is also a yearning for initiation. Something in the adolescent male wants risk, courts danger, goes out to the edge, even to the edge of death.

Everyone knows this tendency of boys to take risks and seek heroism. It makes sense to formalise (and therefore make safer) this craving for physical intensity as a mark of crossing a threshold. There's a real need to be cautious here. Sam Keen points out that the more warlike societies had the crueller initiations – that there is an element of dehumanising the boys from the soft world of their mothers, making them mean. Like so many things, it must involve a fine balance. Perhaps the best equivalents we have are the well-conducted and intense outdoor experiences such as Outward Bound, though something involving men who know and love the boy would also be necessary. (You can't 'purchase' initiation like a father sending his son to school to learn discipline. It never works out.) Whatever is done, the intention must be to empower, to match the experience to the child, never to hurt or humiliate.

False initiation

Many of us remember high school initiations consisting of dunkings and various humiliations. The Australian Military Academy charged a number of its officer trainees with sexual assault on younger men – done in the name of initiation. Perhaps related to this, there have been recent instances in the Navy of quite brutal harassment and rape of women taking up posts on ships – a sign of significant gender insecurity. Lacking real leadership and good initiation, fake initiation arises as an unconscious substitute.

There does need to be toughness in life's transitions – a kind of caesarean delivery is needed. But doing this requires great skill. In a sane society, initiation is the job of the most experienced – it should never be left to the immature.

An initiation he needed like a hole in the head

A man who was shot through the skull with an arrow by a friend trying to knock a fuel can off his head survived with no brain damage. Surgeons removed the arrow from Mr Anthony Roberts' head by drilling a larger hole around the tip at the skull's back, and pulling it through. Mr Roberts was shot on Saturday at the friend's home in Grant's Pass, about 320 km south of Portland. Mr Roberts, an unemployed carpenter, lost his right eye. At a hospital news conference, Mr Roberts initially told reporters he was walking though a park, when he heard a bow fired and then felt the arrow hit. Later he told them his friend was trying to knock the gallon can off his head as part of an initiation into a rafting and outdoor group called Mountain Men Anonymous. Investigators said there was no doubt the can story was true. Mr Roberts said he was drinking with friends when the accident occurred. 'I don't think that's a good initiation,' he said. 'I think a hug would be better.'

If the arrow had been a millimetre closer to his nose, it would have severed major blood vessels, and Mr Roberts could have died on the spot. Dr Delashaw said, 'I've never seen anything like it'.

'I feel really stupid', Mr Roberts said.

A news item from Associated Press

Why does there have to be pain?

The concept of ritual wounding – the purpose it serves and how we recover is complex. We know that a therapist working with a very damaged client has to be incredibly firm and strong. Just low-level kindness will not succeed. If a person has been harmed intensely, they must be loved intensely if they are to release the pain.

Street kids sometimes burn or cut their own skin for a similar reason – the outer pain releases, or is at least more bearable than, the inner pain. Something very strong is needed to unlock the inner pain.

The Men's Movement claims that men are massively wounded in normal life, from birth onwards. Bly lists comprehensively what he calls 'soul wounds':

> Not receiving any blessing from your father is an injury. I waited for two days with my father when he was dying and wanted him to tell me that he loved me. He never did.
>
> Not seeing your father when you are small, never being with him, having a remote father, an absent father, a workaholic father, is an injury ... having a critical, judgmental father ... .
>
> And there are blows from the mother. 'You're too sickly, stay away from those other boys'. 'If you don't stop that I'll send you to a home'. 'You're just like your father'. (Fathers hit with an axe, some mothers poison you slowly with shame.)
>
> Another wound is being lied to – like the old men who sent the young men to Vietnam ... .
>
> Never being made welcome by older men – the ghetto youth are a direct consequence of this.
>
> 'When you look at a gang', Michael Meade remarked, 'you are looking at young men who have no older men around them at all. Gang members try desperately to learn courage, family, loyalty and discipline from each other. It works for a few, but for most it doesn't.'
>
> We can add to the wounding the competitive, unsupportive workplace, where 'the major emotions are anxiety, tension, loneliness, rivalry and fear'. Having no soul union with other men can be the most damaging wound of all. Wounding is inevitable. Being too thin, too fat, short, tall,

big nose, ears, uncoordinated, unmusical and so on. It
doesn't leave many unscathed.

The aim of initiation is a grand one – to put all these hurts
into a meaningful context and turn them into a positive.
When I had (at the age of forty) the great, furious shouting
match I needed to have with my parents, it took place in
an airport carpark. Afterwards, we walked through the
airport concourse and, to my surprise, I was filled with
pride – in all three of us. We had endured. And we had
broken through the pretence that ninety-five percent of
families never break through.

I have, ever since that day, had a delicious sense of
ferocity sitting just behind my eyes, waiting to scorch to a
cinder anyone who is less than real with me. It's rarely
used, but readily available. Nothing short of a full fury
could have released this power from its long sleep.

The wound turns to gold

And there is always something wrong with us. One boy feels
too thin, or too short, or too stringy, another has a stutter
or a limp. One is too shy; another is not 'athletic', or can't
dance or has a bad complexion.

Robert Bly

If your life has been full of difficulty and damage, how can
this be turned to advantage? There is a direct connection
between suffering and greatness. The best therapists and
most outstanding healers are often men and women who
have overcome difficult families, horrible abuse or other
concerted attacks on their psychic and physical being in early
life.

If you want to change the way you are with your sons, and
your daughters, then my experience is you need to feel how
you were hurt, and how you were wounded.

Marvin Allen

We know that the greatest artists, the really great leaders, did not come from bland or cosy suburban lives. They suffered and somehow they 'turned this around'. Of course many other people suffer and simply sink under the weight. Suffering is not a guarantee. But if you have suffered in your life and want to do something about it, one way to start is to begin to think of yourself as lucky!

A close friend of mine is a calm, urbane professional and a family man. He had a father who was quite the opposite – erratic and moody, given to outbursts of sudden violence. My friend recalls being about eight years old and his father asking him to come on a trip. The boy was scared. He hid behind his mother's skirts and did not want to go. While the father yelled and stormed about the house in a rage, the boy went to his bedroom and got into bed. Moments later the father burst into the room, lifted the whole bed and upturned it on top of the boy who was then held beneath it on the floor, screaming on the inside, on the outside silent with terror. It was good that the father didn't kill him, but bad that it happened at all. There were many similar incidents.

When the boy grew up he became a career-driven achiever, yet never felt really happy. Only with the onset of midlife did the pain of these experiences begin to catch up with him – to pour out of his body. He began experiencing all kinds of alarming physical reactions – panic attacks, sensory distortions – but luckily did not panic or run for tranquillisers. Through talking over the experiences, he made the link with his childhood and accessed many memories that had not so much been forgotten as pushed down as too painful. In time, and with help, he became more at ease with himself, able to take better care of himself and emotionally more peaceful and flowing. He also made major career changes, took long holidays with his family and set about a very different rhythm of life based on fulfilment, rather than external achievement.

It's no good toughing it out

'To heal it, you have to feel it.' One of the hardest things for men to admit is that they need help. Yet if you are not helped with the wounds of childhood, then they affect you in two distinctive ways. They can leave you either paralysed and depressed or they can have completely the opposite effect, which is just as bad. They can make you grandiose and over-achieving. You become a compulsive helper of others, always the nice guy who never has a cross word. Interested in the pain of others, without being willing to examine your own pain – 'cheerful, but not very human'.

Bly points out that initiation prevents such a fate, by reframing the wounding into a bigger picture – giving it meaning and channelling its intensity into a positive force. In his words – 'Ancient initiation practice would affect all these responses, since it gives a new wound or gives a calculated wound sufficiently pungent and vivid – though minor – so that the young man remembers his inner wounds. The initiation then tells the young man what to do with wounds, the new and the old.'

In the 'Iron John' story, the young man dips his wounded finger in the pond to soothe its pain. To his amazement, the wounded finger turns to gold! Bly explains:

Turning to gold means all kinds of confidence, freedom and creative flow. The young runner crosses the finish line in the presence of her coach; the tips of her toes are gold. The physicist working with his mentor at Princeton suddenly writes an equation on the board with his golden chalk. Good gardeners have golden thumbs not green thumbs and sometimes the mentor or teacher, sitting with a student, slips into soul water and the tongue turns to gold.

It's a beautiful image, and one that everyone can understand.

Bonding and unbonding in the journey of life

It begins to be clear that initiation isn't a boy scout adventure – or a one-off eco-tourism buzz! (Though that could be a good start!) It's a whole education – taking decades. The sequence of movement from infant to adult man is clear. He moves from:

Mother   to Father   to Mentor   to Manhood.

He must form a trustworthy bond to each in turn, then separate and move on. Each step requires someone adequate to the task to be available which is precisely why for most of us it all goes wrong. In today's world, mothers on the whole are 'there' for their children – though with the trend to long-day care and crèches, even this bonding is endangered. Fathers, on the whole, are the step that fails. Mentors are in even shorter supply. (Older men think they are not needed and wander off to the golf course. Uncles and grandfathers don't realise what they are called upon to do.)

It is very fruitful in rehabilitating your life as a man to first think clearly about how far you have come along this line, then to identify the steps that were missing and then to actively set about filling them – seeking people who *know* what you want to learn. The importance of actively kick-starting your own stalled development in this way cannot be stressed enough.

An Australian initiation

One's traditional roots can often be a good starting point for a modern man seeking personal strength and depth to his life. Whether we are Celtic, Saxon, African, Aboriginal, Asian or whatever, there's a lot of mileage in digging deeper to find which 'powerpoint' you are best plugged-in to. The music, dancing, clothing, customs and landscapes of your native place may well be food for your soul with profound effects on your wellbeing.

In addition to where-you-are-from, there is also the power grid of where-you-are-now. Australia is a country which vibrates with its own character – a character coming largely from the bush. The land itself has the power to make a man whole.

Australia gradually changes all the races who come here. The land shapes the people to suit it. It has had 50 000 years to shape the Aboriginal people who wandered across the land bridge from Asia. It has given them their breathy, musical voices, far-seeing eyes and minds that can grasp the fine details of the landscape. They are perfect for the place.

The same process continues with us, the newcomers. The evergreen vegetation, harsh weather, the vast spaces and long, dry distances reach into us and alter our genes. Perhaps we are all in the process, over generations, of becoming Aboriginal (and the better for it). All of us – Poms, Lebanese, and Asian boat-people – are gradually becoming Aboriginal!

Knowing this might be of some use to Australian men, lost souls that we are. We could save ourselves some time. As we read and search for the keys to manhood, it may pay to learn from Aboriginals, for whom *initiation* has always been a most essential part of life. Not to mimic them but to get some feel for the kind of qualities we are looking for in our own initiation process.

The story of Charles Perkins

The following is adapted, with permission, from an article by Stuart Rintoul in the *Australian* newspaper of February 15, 1992.

Charles Perkins – an Aboriginal and for many years a senior public servant – is known to most Australians. For a time as Head of the Department of Aboriginal Affairs, a graduate in psychology and anthropology and holder of the

Order of Australia, Perkins was *the* Aboriginal repre-
sentative in Canberra. Then the dream collapsed. Falsely
implicated in accusations of mismanaged funds, he felt
deserted and scapegoated by his own minister and by the
Prime Minister, Bob Hawke. Perkins was eventually cleared
of all allegations, but left his public service career in disgust
and returned to Alice Springs.

Then, some years later, in 1990, Perkins did a remarkable
thing. He became formally initiated as a man of the Arunta
people – the clan into which he was born and from which
he was stolen by welfare authorities as a child. It began
quite simply, when an elder confronted him, late one night,
at a campfire meeting in the desert. The old man gave
Perkins a tirade about his life and achievements, ending
with the simple statement of fact – 'There's another world
you don't know properly'. Perkins realised that the old man
was right and that he did not understand the very thing he
was fighting for. He was not a real Aboriginal, because he
had not undergone the process of becoming one. Perkins
accepted the invitation. Here in his own words he conveys,
as well as anyone can, the effect on him of this experience:

> ... it is beyond, I think, your imagination. I could never
> tell anyone, explain what it means; it's just too much and
> nobody knows but me and the people in the ceremonies
> what happened and what it all means. It just boggles the
> mind, it really does.
>
> There are two worlds ... .
>
> You sit there at night, with the fires burning and maybe
> 200 people dancing, it was awe inspiring ... you're going
> back 50 000 years in time. It writes new chapters in your
> brain.

It was not just a personal transformation. Perkins believes
that the way he has gone holds the key to the rehabilitation
of Aboriginal people, away from spiralling poverty, drunk-
enness and violence. Of his life before initiation, he is

quoted as saying he often felt he was watching life, rather than living it:

> Unless you drink the water or suck a few leaves, or kick a stone or smell the flowers, you might as well be living in a movie. When I was living in Canberra I felt that a lot.

(Canberra affects a lot of people like that.) In accordance with tradition, Perkins will say nothing of the actual process. The forms, catalogued by anthropologists, are remarkably consistent throughout the nonliterate world and across aeons of time. They include incisions of the body, long periods of hardship out in the bush, the learning of stories, songs and dances and obedience to elders. Discipline, often hard for others to comprehend, is usually a part of the outcome:

> Our law is strong and there are certain things that happen if you don't observe the law. There are people here that I have known all my life, that I can no longer talk to.

For us to dwell here on the physical process of initiation will not convey much of the inner meaning of the experience. Let's face it, our preconceptions of stages we have not gone through are about as deep as a six-year-old's understanding of sex or a teenager's grasp of growing old. We simply have to accept this and wait to be enlightened. There are some things in life you won't understand without experiencing them and which do not come without effort.

For Perkins, initiation was clearly only the beginning of a lifelong learning process as he learns the language, songs and the path of an Arunta elder. But it's clearly, overwhelmingly worth it.

> When I went through the ceremonies, the world changed. The trees were different, the leaves were different, the grass was different, the hills were different, the air was different. I am looking at a tree and one day it is a tree and the next day it was my friend. I saw somebody else there. I was at home.

Meeting the Wild Man

One way to understand the meaning of initiation is to say that it is 'a journey to meet the Wild Man'. The Wild Man is not easy to explain, although most men can in some way relate to the concept. He is both a being that is *in* men and yet also has independent life. He both represents – and teaches us – our own brilliance, bounty, wildness, greatness and spontaneity. The Wild Man teaches that we don't have to pretend to be good, but that we have power and integrity latent inside us, if we trust it. Abandoning yourself to wildness turns out to be the most harmonious and generative thing you can do. (Fans of Taoism and Lao Tsu will feel right at home here.) When we are good, we are okay, but when we are 'wild' we are geniuses. Any man who makes or builds things, who creates a garden, who plays a jazz instrument, who has ever been a lover, knows that you are better when you 'let go' and follow your impulses. Natural rhythms within us take over and bring out our real talents.

Our love of trees, the outback, waves and water, animals, growing things, music, children and women, all stem from our wild nature. The most creative men are close to the Wild Man and borrow his power.

> The aim is not to *be* the wild man, but to be in touch with the wild man.
>
> Robert Bly

All masculine confidence, of the inner kind, arises in the domain of the Wild Man. Also the way to develop male spirituality is to 'know' the Wild Man – to converse with him, not to become him. (Jesus, Mohammed, Buddha were well at ease with the Wild Man – spending time in the wilderness, using nature as their place of prayer and reflection. All bore his hallmarks – being unpredictable and nonconformist with the established order of their times, yet at the same time disciplined and true to their inner voices.)

The Wild Man aspect of the Men's Movement is often

pounced on by the media looking for sensational content –
the seemingly ridiculous idea of weekend warriors leaping
about and banging drums in the forest. But no-one who
experiences these things is likely to joke about them. In her
wonderful book, *Women Who Run With The Wolves*, C.P.
Estes recommends precisely the same to women – that they
need a civilised part and a wild intuitive part, in balance.
The over-civility of women – excessive niceness – endangers
them, just as much as it does men.

Bly states forcefully that wild does not mean savage:

> The savage mode does great damage to soil, earth and
> humankind; we can say that though the savage man is
> wounded he prefers not to examine it. The Wild Man who
> has examined his wound resembles a Zen priest, a shaman
> or a woodsman more than a savage.

We have to learn to trust that our original nature, our inner
self, is good. To be convinced of this you have only to look
closely at a baby. Clearly we are all born beautiful. This is
why birth is so moving. Wordsworth was right – we come
to earth 'trailing clouds of glory'. Bly says, 'The child is
the inheritor of millenia of spiritual and imaginative labour.
The aim is to rediscover this, through initiation. You get
hooked up to the grid'.

> It is good that the divine is associated with the Virgin Mary
> and a blissful Jesus, but we can sense how different it
> would be for young men if we lived in a culture where the
> divine also was associated with mad dancers, fierce-fanged
> men and a being entirely underwater, covered with hair.
>
> Robert Bly

The Wild Man

How do we contact the Wild Man to restore life and health
to ourselves as men? One writer, Asa Baber, described this
so well that I will quote him at length.

Robert Bly presents a precise summation of what has happened to many men over the past three decades – when the feminist revolution has taken over the culture and told us how terrible we were as men and how much we needed to change. To be macho in any manner has become unfashionable. And yet, every man has an element of macho in his genetic structure. To deny it and suppress it can be deadly to men (and to the culture). Such denial can leave us depressed, without energy or passion or identity.

As men we have special gifts. One of these is the ability to be in touch with the Cro-Magnon man who lives somewhere deep inside our hearts and minds and calls to us. It is vital to remember that this man is not a savage. In no way is he an uncontrolled killer or evil oppressor. He is primordial, but not barbaric, aboriginal, but not vicious. He represents what is best in the spirit of manhood. Indomitable and invincible and wild, ready to protect and defend and compete, his instinct and perceptions necessary to ensure the survival of the human race, this primitive man at the center of our psyches must be allowed room to live and breathe and express himself. If this rudimentary part of us dies, male identity dies.

Bly, borrowing a term from 'Iron John' an ancient fairy tale collected by the Grimm Brothers, calls this primitive man 'the wildman'. It is not a bad name for him.

In 'Iron John', a young man on a difficult journey sees a large hairy creature at the bottom of a pond that the young man is emptying bucket by bucket (this story is replete with symbols). This discovery is frightening and intriguing. 'What I'm proposing', says Bly, 'is that every modern male, has lying at the bottom of his psyche, a large primitive man covered with hair down to his feet. Making contact with this wild man is the process that still hasn't taken place in contemporary culture. Freud, Jung and Wilhelm Reich are three men who had the courage to go down into the pond and accept what's there. The job of modern males is to follow them down.'

Accepting what is dark down there – what he calls 'the shadow' – is another task that Bly assigns to any man who would discover his true male self and become an initiated male. Under Bly's urging, men are beginning to explore this shadow side of their personalities. Anger, aggression, grief, feelings of abandonment and rejection, rage, confusion – all the varied dark and shadowy forces that whirl around like demons in the male psyche – these are things we have tried to deny or ignore in order to be acceptable and admired.

But we have tried much too hard to be nice and we have essentially handed over the job of self-definition to others. This turns out to have been self-destructive. We emasculate and feminise ourselves to gain female approval and then we hope against all available evidence that our masculine energies will leave us alone. But is that likely?

Face it: For most men, the hope that our energy will fade away is in vain. Witness the fact that our sexuality emerges at a very early age – and carries with it a beautiful immediacy, from spontaneous erections to wet dreams and vivid fantasies. This immediacy of male sexuality lasts well into our adulthood, even into old age for many men. Are we really going to be able to suppress all of that energy? And why should we repudiate such a unique and wonderful drive?

To use a Bly analogy, 'The Widow Douglas wanted Huck Finn to be nice. And after he has floated down the river with the black man, Aunt Sally wants to adopt him and "civilise" him. Huck says, "I can't stand it. I been there before."' Sounds familiar, doesn't it.

The wildman lives in every man. He is beautiful and divine. He has enormous fundamental energy and a great love for the world. He is just as much a nurturer and protector and creator as any female figure, but he will do that nurturing and protecting in his own masculine way. It is time for the Wild Man in us to be celebrated without shame. That celebration is part of what our revolution is about. It is our job as men to know ourselves better so that we can

contribute more to this world and be more honest with ourselves. We have a right to our revolution, in other words.
An absolute right.

Asa Baber in Wingspan

Wildness as the home of man

For some, the above will sound rather esoteric. Put in
simple terms: Why do men love to go bush? And why is it
that the wisest, most solid and most trustworthy men we
all know are also the ones who love fishing or gardening,
bushwalking, the sea, the weather – men who find some
excuse or other to spend time in wild places?

The reason is clear. Out there – in the wind, under the
stars and in the crash of waves – is where they find
invigorating communion with the Wild Man. It seems obvious, and yet whole generations of children grow up without
entering a forest, touching a wild creature, or ever sleeping
under the stars. We must not forget how closely linked to
sanity these experiences are:

> Iron John wants the young man to experience the garden.
> Once the garden – which may take ten years to develop –
> has been experienced, then we could say that the young
> man has learned to honor his own soul, has learned to
> become a lover and has learned to dance.

Robert Bly

Venus Bay – edge of the wild

When I was about fourteen, our family visited a place called
Venus Bay. We were a close-knit family, in that deathly
English kind of way, and in our new country as social
isolates things were getting to the pressure-cooker stage!
Family drives and camping trips were welcome breaks from
the monotony of day-to-day life. I include this background

to set a kind of mood to my adolescence that is important to the story:

> This particular day dawned sunny and perfectly still. We had the place to ourselves and walked by the water's edge, just taking it all in. The Australian coastline still has places where the forest runs down to the sea and a sense of wild nature pervades. After we had gone a kilometre or two along the sea edge, I decided to go for a swim and walked into the trees behind the dunes for a private place to change into my bathers. Standing with my clothes off, in a glade of sunlight among twisted tea-tree and vines, I was aware of a combination – my body unfamiliarly naked, warm sunlight on my pale skin and a smell of honeysuckle. Half-lit glades festooned with creepers lay all around. There was a sense of total, primal wildness that was seductive, welcoming and mysterious all at the same time. Sexuality was in there along with other more global feelings. At that moment I simply felt more alive than I had ever recalled feeling in my whole life. I could have run off into that forest and never returned.

This feeling of profound connection is every child's birthright. We should be able to build our life around it. All art, music, religion, poetry, is an attempt to return to it. It is at the heart of what we seek in lovemaking. Yet it is the very opposite of what we build around ourselves in the modern world.

Robert Bly puts it very bluntly: 'If you are a man', he says, 'civilisation will kill you.' American Indian people shared the same reaction when they saw with horror the white man's cities and towns. The Amazon people say it today. They don't so much fear the white man's world, rather they are horrified by its toxicity to a man's soul. They look at our world and pity us.

Like millions of men, I love to spend time in the bush, despite the effort, discomfort and sometimes danger involved. This need is the very same one that drives the worldwide movement to conserve wilderness. There are good, practical arguments – as basic as the world's oxygen supply and profound as the species and substances which may hold the secret to cancer treatment or agricultural survival – but these are not the real reason people love the wilderness. It's because their hearts feed on its existence. To go into those places from and taste the wildness, that is what keeps us sane. It is our connection to God. Man's cathedrals only mimic the arches and dappled sunlight of the forest. Our music only echoes the sound of wind and birds. Drugs simulate the rush and exhilaration of being alive in such places. Alcohol copies the relaxation and brotherhood of being exhausted in the business of just staying alive in the bush with friends. But all are poor substitutes for the real thing.

Even the schizophrenic Japanese culture, tearing the Pacific rim apart to feed a consumerist madness, still takes refuge in the bonsai tree or the pebble garden. Even the 1950s' suburbanite has his three ducks on the wall!

The Trickster

There are other 'beings' in the soul of man, along with the Wild Man. One of these is the Trickster (the 'Coyote Man' of North American Indians). Jungian psychology points out that we have not one personality, but a dialogue of parts which need to be kept in balance. You **need** to have in you a Trickster – the sneaky, playful individualist who owes nothing to anyone. This part is very useful for keeping you out of fundamentalism of any kind. (It's always the fundamentalists who want to kill and imprison and start world wars.) Not just fundamentalist religion, but any mindless following without questioning of an 'ism'. 'Isms' are dangerous and divisive and we need to know when to drop them. The Trickster has no respect, which is often useful! Anyone who is too intense, too rigid, anyone who is caught up in something, needs more Trickster:

If you have a compulsive tendency to blush, then you probably need to work in integrating your Trickster, because he doesn't get embarrassed so easily.

Robert Moore in *Wingspan*

On the other hand you can have too much Trickster. Robert Moore says this: 'If you have a friend who is a very, very cynical individual, his Trickster is on automatic. Ask him to tell you about the men he admires. And if he cannot list his masculine saints who function for him in his life, then his Trickster is on pretty full automatic. You show me a man who has no men who he admires and I'll show you a man whose Trickster is running over all the time.'

You need a set of saints, especially male saints if you are a man. These are based on real people, but their ideal has its own life inside you. We build our own identity by borrowing that of others. (I got through my mid-teens by emulating the hero in the Kung Fu series. Not in drop-kicking baddies, but learning to be kind instead of bitter, appreciating early the value of meditation. My loneliness was given some nobility and purpose. Until more flesh and blood mentors come along, we all need our heroes.) Men who reject heroes are not like that by accident. They have often been so mistreated by older men that they have generalised that all men are abusive. They need help to learn that not all men will harm them, and that tenderness and vulnerability can be positives. Cynicism, after all, is immobilising and precludes taking strong action.

The ancient Greeks understood how these archetypes worked. They had many temples and many gods and knew how to access the right god for the right stage of life. For instance, a woman who had been disappointed in love could go to the temple of Diana. She would live and learn with hardy, athletic huntress women, who valued female strength and needed nothing of men. She might worship there for a year or more. Entering another phase of her life, she might worship Aphrodite. Later as a wife and mother she would worship in the temple of Hera. The sequence was flexible, each venue aided the individual in a rich and sound progression.

So, for the Greeks, life always had a sacred dimension. Every stage of life was codified and respected. Bly compares this with our culture of randomness: 'They went from temple to temple, we just stagger from one McDonalds to the next!'

The time of Ashes

Have you ever seen the look in the eyes of a thirty-five-year-old man?

Robert Bly

Young men need to fall before they can rise. We are taught that adolescence is the big transition of life, but given no information about other important journeys. Most of us get through our adolescence, give a big sigh of relief and assume we've made it! But there are even bigger changes awaiting the adult male. No-one is even close to being a fully-grown male before they turn forty.

Young men, in their late teens and twenties, are cocky. They have an optimism which is charming but shallow – since it has never been tested. They are inclined to think they are invincible. Eventually though, all men learn that not everything works out in this life. The mid-thirties seem to be the time that this often happens. The trigger can be anything. Perhaps a baby is stillborn. Or your wife stops loving you. A once-sturdy father shrivels and dies before your eyes. A lump becomes cancerous. A car accident smashes up your body. Or your carefully built career tumbles like a pack of cards. Suddenly there is shame, error and grief all around you. Welcome to the Ashes.

In my mid-thirties, the trigger for my journey downwards was a miscarriage – an abrupt end to a much-wanted pregnancy. When my partner felt the contractions after only three months of pregnancy, I swung into auto-pilot – being the caring and competent husband. I drove us to hospital calmly and safely. I remember standing with her, soaking in the shower room at the hospital, catching in my wet hands small pieces of our hoped-for child. Still seemingly unaffected, I carried off a two-day seminar straight after the event. Then the impact came. I sank slowly into a black hole that lasted for six months. To this day I barely understand what happened. I can only guess that my sense of optimism and confidence evaporated in the face of powerless grief. I became unlovable, self-absorbed, barely wanting to get out of bed. My moods served only to push away my partner, who was handling her own grief. I drifted towards non-being.

Somehow, gradually, as time went on, I softened inside. I was so confused, and on unfamiliar ground, which meant a good thing started to happen. I had to swallow my pride and let friends help me – which for me was not easy. Gradually, over time, I rebuilt a sense of self that incorporated a new understanding. What I now know is that I am like everyone else – totally weak, totally vulnerable, lucky that life tests my limits so rarely, lucky just to be alive. In a word, humbled.

You do not have to experience total devastation in order to grow into a mature man, but you have to know its possibility deep in your bones – to discover that you are not all-powerful and your dreams may well not come true. Thus you make the journey down into Ashes, perhaps many times. (If you fail to learn the lesson the first time, then down you go again!) Finally you get the message and only then do you go from being a careless boy to a more open-hearted and compassionate man.

Nations need Ashes too

Whole countries need to go through this maturation, unless they are to stay perpetual adolescents. Russia is now facing the Ashes of its awful pollution, its alcoholism, the horrendous inefficiencies of its economic system. When America failed to wear the Ashes of Vietnam – electing Reagan and pretending it never happened – then the veterans themselves had to do the Ashes work for a whole nation. It was more than many could bear. Somebody needed to say, 'we're sorry – we were wrong.' But it didn't happen.

For Australia the Mabo and Treaty initiatives with the Aboriginal people are important Ashes work. It's for *our own* sakes that this matters – we cannot build a just nation on theft and murder. Yet still people resist 'wearing' this clear obligation, which any five-year-old child can see the justice of.

> It's sad that the United States still stubbornly refuses to pick up the ashes we have created in the last four decades. Our agricultural policy is ashes, our schools are ashes, the treatment of blacks is all ashes, the trade deficit is ashes, the environmental policy is ashes, the poverty of women and children is ashes.
>
> Robert Bly

Healing through healthy shame

An old man and a younger man are on a long camping trip across the desert. For several days the young man is somewhat tense and quiet. The older man notices this but does not press the point. Finally the younger man begins to talk. He is the manager of a fruit-growing property, and, in the winter twelve months ago, backed a tractor over his own three-year-old son's legs. Disaster was narrowly avoided – the ground was muddy and wet, and the toddler's legs were pressed down into the mud. Miraculously, he was only bruised and shocked.

The young man had been distraught for weeks. Close friends and family told him not to worry, it could have happened to anyone. He recovered somewhat, but he could not put the incident out of his mind. Even on this trip, a much-needed break, he was still experiencing flashbacks and cold sweats. The old man was silent. He did not reassure or minimise the feelings of the young man, who sat also silent, feeling the familiar knotting in his gut as he once again relived the experience.

'Exactly what did people say to you?' the older man asked eventually.

'They said it was an accident. Not to blame myself.'

'Hmmm.' The old man was quiet again for a while.

'They're wrong then,' he said all of a sudden, so that the young man was jolted from his reverie.

'Wh – what do you mean?' he asked.

'It was a really stupid thing to do,' said the old man. 'You're lucky your young fella wasn't flattened'.

The young man was suddenly glad it was dark around their small campfire. His face flushed suddenly, and hot tears began to run down his cheeks.

'I thought my wife was looking after him. We'd just had a fight. I started the tractor. I never looked. I was thinking, it's her bloody job to keep the kids inside, and I never looked.'

By now the older man was alongside the younger one, gripping his shoulder with one hand. The young man simply pitched forwards onto the sand, wailing out loud. The older man moved alongside him and put one hand on his arm. The young man seemed to continue his curving fall into the old man's chest, holding on and sobbing great, gulping sobs. After a time the sobbing stopped. He became aware of the texture of the older man's shirt against his cheek, sat up a little, and looked at the starry desert sky over his shoulder. A deep calmness settled into him; calmer than he had ever felt.

The grief that makes us whole

The benefits of things going badly:

It is said whenever a friend reported enthusiastially, 'I've just been promoted', Jung would say, 'I'm very sorry to hear that; but if we stick together I think we will get through it'. If a friend arrived depressed and ashamed, saying, 'I've just been fired', Jung would say, 'Let's open a bottle of wine; this is wonderful news. Something good will happen now.'

... some power in the psyche arranges a severe katabasis if the man does not know enough to go down on his own.

Depression is a small katabasis, and something other than us arranges it. Depression usually surprises us by its arrival and its departure. In depression, we refuse to go down and so a hand comes up and pulls us down. In grief, we choose to go down.

To receive initiation, truly, means to expand sideways into the glory of oaks, mountains, glaciers, horses, lions, grasses, waterfalls, deer. **We** need wilderness and extravagance. Whatever shuts a human being away from the waterfall and the tiger will kill him.

The wild man's job is to teach the young man how abundant, various and many-sided his manhood is. The job of the initiator is to prove to the boy or girl that he or she is more than mere flesh and blood. ... each carries desires far beyond what is needed for mere survival.

... he learned that the whole world is on fire. 'Everything is intelligent!'

Robert Bly

Every man needs an Ashes time in his life. To discover that, in spite of all optimism and effort, one is still vulnerable. To fall into despair at these times, though very inviting, is to miss the point. Grief is cleansing, despair is just standing still. The key is to *let your feelings out*.

Life is about going on, being active, making decisions, taking steps in this life, not knowing how it will work out. Life is a tough business. If a man is able at these times to allow himself to cry and share some of his pain with his friends, then he comes through a better man. He no longer looks disdainfully at poor, handicapped or weak people. He realises that they are just like him. His capacity for compassion deepens enormously. The Ashes time completes what has begun in adolescence – the making of a real man.

In a nutshell

1 Have a think about where you are going. What you will do when your children are gone, and your wife is dead. What is your life about – when there is just you?

2 Create a space for yourself that is separate, so you can get to know yourself apart from your roles.

3 Realise that for men, nature is where your home is. Spend time there. Pursue wildness – especially if you live in the city. Take deliberate action – like walking on the beach – so that you can reattune yourself to the rhythms of earth, ocean and sky.

4 Be religious. Expecially favour religions that dance, bang drums, sing or sit in total silence.

5 Take a year off when you turn forty, and do things you have postponed, or always wanted to do. Reevaluate whether you wish to continue in the way you have been going, or make changes.

6 Each year, around the time of your birthday, spend four days (minimum) in complete solitude.

7 Think about whether you need some kind of initiation into manhood – to move from being a perpetual adolescent.

8 Learn about the ancient culture of the land you live on. For Australians, the Aboriginal culture, mood and temperament will be very instructive.

9 Accept times of great misfortune – a marriage breakdown, sickness or business failure – as essential
steps to getting free. Roll in the Ashes. Don't be
afraid of pain, grief, sadness, weakness or failure.
They enrich your humanness.

10 Go looking for the Wild Man.

Other voices

- Some men enter the garden by getting up at 5 a.m. and keeping an hour for themselves each morning before work. A father, in order to do this, may have to resist his own insistence that his life belongs to his work, his children and his marriage.

  Robert Bly in *Wingspan*

- The older men who still today initiate boys in Australian Aborigine tribes, and in New Guinea and in African tribes, take the boys away from the mothers between the ages of eight and twelve, and begin a complicated sequence of adventures, teachings, trials and dances. The old men recite poems, act out myths, say outrageous things, and may themselves dance all night. The boys experience close-up what the emotional body of a man is like when it is activated. The boys in some African tribes are taught to dance all night for twenty-four hours straight.

  Robert Bly in *Wingspan*

- Why should I flail about with words, when love has made the space inside me full of light?

  Kabir

- We gain personal authority and find our unique sense of self only when we learn to distinguish between our own story, our autobiographical truths and the official myths that have previously governed our minds, feelings and actions. This begins when we ask, 'What story have I been living? What myth has captured me?' It ends only when we tell our own story and authorise our own lives ... .

  Robert Bly in *To Be a Man*

- The Wild Man doesn't come to full life through being 'natural', going with the flow, smoking weed, reading nothing and

being generally groovy. Ecstasy amounts to living within
reach of the high voltage of the golden gifts. The ecstasy
comes after thought, after discipline imposed on ourselves,
after grief.

Robert Bly

• Despite our Disneyland culture, some men around thirty-five
or forty will begin to experience ashes privately, without
ritual, even without old men. They begin to notice how many
of their dreams have turned to ashes. A young man in high
school dreams that he will be a race driver, a mountain climb-
er, he will marry Miss America, he will be a millionaire by
thirty, he will get a Nobel Prize in physics by thirty-five, he
will be an architect and build the tallest building ever. He
will get out of this hick town and live in Paris. He will have
fabulous friends ... and by thirty-five, all these dreams are
ashes.
The recognition of this diminishment is a proper experience
for a man over thirty. If the man doesn't experience that
diminishment sharply, he will retain his inflation and continue to identify himself with all in him that can fly – his
sexual drive, his mind, his refusal to commit himself, his
addiction, his transcendence, his coolness. The coolness of
some American men means they have skipped ashes.

Robert Bly

• The Gold Woman in the other world sends her radiance down
through the atmosphere, and the radiance appears on the
girl's face. Her beauty is a good enough hook for the boy's
otherworldly longing, perhaps she even fits some template in
their genetic memory. They take one look and summer is complete.

Robert Bly

Shaking Free
Male toilet facilities are ripe for liberation, according to
Walker Feinlein, Professor of Gender Ergonomics at the Univer-
sity of Hobart.

Women, said Professor Feinlein, would never tolerate the barbaric conditions men have to endure in toileting. 'Go in there and have a look for yourself', he tells his female students. Standing at a communal receptacle (known in architectural circles as a pisseteria), men suffer all kinds of social awkwardness and competitive trauma.

A second serious problem is 'drip retention syndrome'. 'Genital physiology and small-droplet physics dictate that no man can ever quite shake dry the male organ – or to use a classic quote:

'No matter how you shake and squeeze,
the last drop goes in your BVD's.'
[*A generic brand of underpants*]

Or in the words of Robbie Burns:
'No matter how much ye shake yer peg
The last wee drap rins doon yer leg.'

The result is that by lunchtime on an average day, most men smell like a pub toilet from the waist down. It's a big problem, and wearing kilts is really just avoiding the issue!

Provision of toilet paper for men, and somewhere to dispose of it, together with more widespread acceptance of drying behaviour, would be welcomed by men and their womenfolk, and spell the end of dark trousers.

Reported in *Chips*, the journal of the Tasmanian Forestry Commission

• Some men who fail to rescue their mothers become therapists and attempt to rescue a woman over and over. They bite off the finger of their emotions, and listen to other people's emotions the rest of their lives.

Robert Bly

• Friendship in certain subsections within Australia amounts almost to religion. This closeness and sharing is not describable to any other cultural group to whom friendship means dinner parties, where one discusses wittily work and career,

or gatherings of 'interesting' people who are all suspicious,
wary and terrified of not being interesting after all ...

Robyn Davidson in Tracks

- Some readers will remember Kafka's story about the doorkeeper and the supplicant. The supplicant waits by the door
  for months, for years, waiting for the moment the door
  opens or when the doorkeeper falls asleep or when he will
  be invited in. Years pass. Finally when old and dying he
  calls the doorkeeper over and whispers to him about the
  injustice of it all. The doorkeeper says, 'Oh, this was your
  door; you could have gone through at any moment'. And the
  supplicant dies.

Robert Bly in Wingspan

12
Men's Groups

Hopefully, reading this book has given you some good ideas for your own life, which you may have already begun to implement. But perhaps you are feeling a little overwhelmed. One problem with the whole 'self-help' and 'self-improvement' scene is the expectation that we can change things all on our own. Twentieth century man has been plagued by this illusion. When this solitary approach fails, we conclude that nothing can be changed after all, and give up. So today, most young men are brashly over confident, and most older men are depressed!

Since writing the first edition of *Manhood*, I have learned some things about the importance of having a male community. To make personal change easier, and to make global change possible, we have to build and belong to a community of men who are working towards similar goals. Even small groups of men who are willing to meet regularly and talk, can give each other enormous insights, enormous amounts of encouragement, and occasional kicks in the bum – all essential to keeping you open and moving towards liberation! If you want your life as a man to really get moving, then you could probably get a lot out of a men's group. Here are some guidelines if you are interested.

The growth of men's groups

In a lounge room not far from where you are reading this, its odds on that a group of eight or nine men are meeting every couple of weeks to talk about their lives. Their wives or partners are happy to vacate the house on that night, because they like the results – a happier, more balanced, stronger and more peaceful man.

We know of several hundred men's groups in Australia; there are doubtless many more quietly getting on with it. Overseas the picture is the same. Therapist-turned-activist Guy Corneau has singlehandedly founded 300 groups in Canada; there are thousands in the US. In the UK, Germany, South America and New Zealand, men's groups are forming, writing newsletters, 'internetting', holding conferences and getting excited. Different emphases are emerging: in the US there are special efforts being made by ghetto groups, and men of different races. In Australia good links are being forged with Aboriginal people, and major focuses are the mentoring of adolescent boys and helping fathers do their jobs.

As with every new movement the media is only just starting to comprehend its significance and is now moving on from simplistic stereotyping. (The Women's Movement and Conservation Movements came in for the same treatment.) The Men's Movement has been lampooned for its inwardness, even for its emotionality. One TV network regularly reused a piece of video footage to represent men's gatherings. It showed a man in deep grief, supported by some other men. He had just acknowledged the sexual abuse he suffered as a child and the hurt he still carried. Yet it was presented as if it was some Californian executive indulging himself for the sake of it. It's typical of the way we set men up – go to war, survive divorce, be a policeman, pull children's bodies out of mangled cars, but don't tell us about your grief.

How men's groups work

Men's groups can be emotional at times. Something very freeing happens when a private space is set aside, when the rules are 'no bullshitting', and 'say what you feel'. 'If men know their stories will be heard and honoured, then a great deal finds its way to the surface.

Men's groups are also very practical. The chosen topic of the night may be 'how to discipline your kids', or 'how to break out of an alienating career and make time to live'. It might be some frank discussion about sex, or it might be more crisis-driven – shoring up a man wounded from marital combat, or a man whose wife has just that week been diagnosed with cancer. I've listened in men's groups to older men talk about war trauma, honestly, for the first time after decades of silent suffering.

Young men find surrogate fathers and uncles in the group, to replace the absent drones their real fathers appeared to be. The ethics of men's groups are strong – particularly about never acting (or even speaking) violently to women, children or each other. Men's-group talk has a style that is very different to women's talk – there's less tiptoeing, and less tendency to agree with everything you say.

Men's groups usually meet in homes, occasionally they are church-based or in a health centre. Most are general purpose, some are specifically for men with violence problems or health or marital concerns. A group may close its membership once it is running, though some will invite new members periodically. The commonest way to start is to invite a few friends and begin your own. Some groups use a book (such as this one) as a discussion starter or generate a list of topics agreed by members. Leadership tends to be rotated, rather than having no leader at all – acknowledging that men like structure and are goal oriented. Men's groups usually have rules (no put-downs, confidentiality) and there is a tendency to confront bullshit or irresponsibility. 'You're neglecting your bloody kids mate ! When are you going to wake up to yourself !' – 'Well, sure you could leave your wife, but you'd be an idiot to do it. Why don't you talk to her and tell her what you're feeling.' 'You're tired, mate. You and your wife need a holiday.' And so on. You don't have to 'spill your guts' in a men's group – there isn't any pressure. Perhaps for that very reason, though, you soon find yourself hoeing in – prompted by the similarities of your own experiences with those being shared by the other men. You get practical tips for living and feel you can breathe more deeply, all at the same time! It adds a sense of relaxation to your life – (quite different to getting drunk or going fishing) because the changes are cumulative. Your life starts to make more sense.

Most men's groups reach a point where they organise to get away for weekends. Also in groups where most men are fathers, activities are often planned to include the youngsters. Some groups, such as YMCA Explorers, exist specifically for dads and daughters, or dads and sons, to spend time together supported by some resources and structure.

Where this may lead

What about the big picture? In time the Men's Movement will lead to legislative and workplace changes. Our economy and the wider world will be affected in many ways. (A national newsletter is advertised in the back of this book). People will consider other necessary changes: the way that boys are treated in schools; the access situation for fathers; exploitation of young men in sport, sexual abuse and exploitation of boys, men in the military; the situation in prisons; the right of children to have and know their fathers; and the prevention of rape and harassment of women. The field is wide.

In a sense, the Men's Movement is a vital missing piece in this jig-saw of human change. Who knows where it might take us ? If you're a man, you're part of it and your actions will make a difference. If you're a woman reading this, we ask for your support and welcome your input.

Warmest wishes

Steve Biddulph
Coffs Harbour
Spring, 1995.

In a nutshell

1 The 'self-made man' is a myth – we all need the help of others to make and sustain change.

2 Join a men's group, or start one with friends.

3 Groups that succeed usually have a structure or program, and rotate leadership to keep direction and purpose.

4 A planet-wide movement for men's liberation and betterment is gathering momentum. Just in the nick of time!

Future Dreaming

What will change as a result of the men's movement?

Men in the future will . . .

Work less, play more. Earn less, spend less. Parent more, stay married longer. Live longer. Be safer to be around.

They will also . . .

Have more friends, and be closer to those friends.
Watch less sport and play more sport.
Take a long term interest in outdoor and wilderness pursuits, of a quieter and more experiential kind.
Become almost religious about, quietly dedicated to, ecological activism.

As lovers they will . . .

Be better in bed, more alive in their bodies, but also more confident, less needy, more friendly – in less of a hurry.

As fathers men will . . .

be involved and positive, and willing to take a firm stand, without being carping or intimidating.

As consumers they will . . .

Dress more warmly and colourfully. Wear handmade and decorative but distinctively masculine clothes and artefacts. (The suit, and tie will disappear. Like the cummerbund and the frock coat, they will become historical oddities.)
Drive old but classy cars, and look after them.
Learn to play more musical instruments.

Prefer 'world' music and move away from youth-oriented styles or products.

The cult of youth will disappear, and young people will be seen as they are, lovely but immature, and certainly not to be envied.

Old age and experience will swiftly be revalued in everything from fashion, movies, employment trends and leadership choices.

Role-models will be people in their fifties and older, especially men and women of a warm and unhurried kind, yet still prickly and confronting, authoritative and humorous.

Existing religions will be revitalised as men take a greater interest in their inner world;

and, in addition, new hybrids and forms of ceremony will be evolved – especially those helping men to heal their pasts and to initiate their teenage sons. A gradual blurring of religion and ecology will begin to emerge as a power in its own right.

Many men will, as a kind of ritual choice, take their fortieth year off from work and pursue other goals.

They will then decide whether to continue in their career or make changes.

Most men will also spend a few days each year, around the time of their birthdays, in complete solitude.

Locally organised and well trained groups of men will confront and work with child-abusers, rapists and wife-beaters, in caring but extremely tough monitoring networks and self-help groups. This will save police resources for more white-collar crime work!

Men will organise themselves and work alongside women in the community, developing vastly different political and activist organisations, tackling local and global issues, using a myriad of computer networks, faxes and newsletters.

They will alter the face of schools, rewrite the whole nature of childhood, wrest local councils back from business inter-ests, demolish traditional political parties, and work and network with developing countries and native people to learn from them more about how to live, love and heal on this planet.

In a sense, you won't have to choose whether to 'join' the men's movement, because it includes all men.

It will be as natural as breathing.

Steve Biddulph, 1995

Relating with Respect

The two wheels – 'Power and Control' and 'Equality' – used in the Duluth Domestic Abuse Intervention Project give a comprehensive view of how men often use power tactics in their relationships with women instead of relating on an equal footing.

Power and control

Study the segments on the left-hand wheel, to determine if you ever use such methods to 'get your way'. Look at the corresponding segments on the right-hand wheel to find the alternative methods, based on respect and communication.

Men who use power tactics often deny that they are doing so. The wheels, when used in the Duluth-style group programs, leave little doubt. If you use this behaviour, you are using power tactics. From this admission, your peers and leaders will help you to find better ways.

Equality

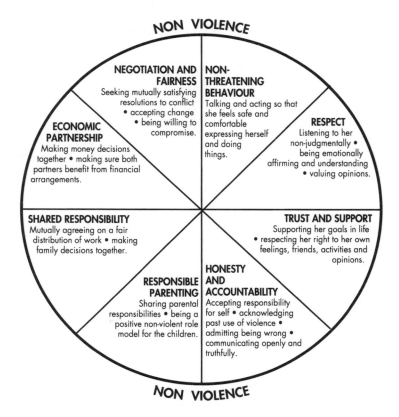

In those U.S. states where the Duluth model has been adopted, it is used as part of the judicial process. Participation is mandatory. Assaultive behaviour is always prosecuted in the courts.

Power tactics are not solely the preserve of men. Women may find that they also use some of the quadrants, and may wish to shift to more equal relating. The Duluth model also provides for spouse programs to assist women in breaking the cycle of violence.

The benefit of giving up power and control is a vastly better life with respect, affection and safety replacing the old patterns. Most men would rather be loved and respected than feared and hated by their wives and children. With models like this, combining male-to-male confrontation and education, we now know how to bring this about.

Bibliography

Books quoted in the text

BLANKENHORN, DAVID *Fatherless America* Basic Books, New York, 1995.

BLY, ROBERT *Iron John: A Book About Men*, Element, London, 1991.

DALBEY, GORDEN *Healing the Masculine Soul*, Word, Melbourne, 1989.

ELIUM, DON AND JEANNE *Raising a Son*, Beyond Words, California, 1992.

EMBLING, JOHN *Fragmented Lives: A darker side of Australian life*, Penguin, Melbourne, 1986.

GOLDBERG, HERB *The New Male*, Bantam, New York, 1984.

HAGAN, KAY LEIGH (editor) *Women Respond to the Men's Movement*, Pandora/HarperCollins, San Francisco, 1993.

HARDING, CHRISTOPHER (editor) *Wingspan – Inside the Men's Movement*, St Martins Press, New York, 1992.

JONES, CAROLINE *The Search for Meaning (3)*, ABC/Collins Dove, Sydney, 1992.

KEEN, SAM *Fire in the Belly*, Bantam, New York, 1992.

LEE, JOHN *At My Father's Wedding*, Bantam, New York, 1991.

MIEDZIAN, MYRIAM *Boys Will Be Boys*, Virago, London, 1992.

RHODES, RICHARD *Making Love*, Simon & Schuster, New York, 1992.

THOMPSON, KEITH (editor) *To Be a Man: In Search of the Deep Masculine*, Jeremy Tarcher, Los Angeles, 1991.

Articles quoted in the text

ALLEN, MARVIN from the documentary 'Wild Man Weekend', SBS Television.

ASSOCIATED PRESS 'An initiation he needed like a hole in the head', The Mercury.

BALDWIN, JAMES quoted in *To Be a Man* (Keith Thompson).

BLISS, SHEPHERD cited in *Wingspan* (Keith Thompson).

BLY, ROBERT Bloomsbury Review, January, 1991.

CAMUS, ALBERT quoted in *To Be a Man* (Keith Thompson).

COONEY, BARRY 'Touching the Masculine Soul', in *Wingspan* (Christopher Harding).

FEINLEIN, PROF. WALKER p.comm. over counter-lunch at the Black Buffalo Hotel, North Hobart.

FOLLET, KEN from *Night Over Water*, quoted by Barry Oakley, the *Australian Magazine*.

FRIEDAN, BETTY 'The Second Stage', 1981, cited in *Wingspan* (Christopher Harding).

GILLETTE, DOUGLAS 'Men and Intimacy', in *Wingspan* (Christopher Harding).

HARDING, CHRIS 'Men's Secret Societies, 1890s-1990s', in *Wingspan* (Christopher Harding).

HAYWARD, FREDRIC 'Male Bashing', originally appeared in *To Be a Man* (Keith Thompson).

LAWRENCE, D.H. *Women in Love*, quoted by Barry Oakley in the *Australian Magazine*.

LAWRENCE, D.H. 'Healing', from *The Collected Poems of D.H. Lawrence* quoted in *Iron John* (Robert Bly).

LEUNIG, MICHAEL 'The Demon', from *A Bunch of Poesy*, Angus & Robertson/HarperCollins, Sydney, 1992.

LEUNIG, MICHAEL interviewed by Caroline Jones in *The Search for Meaning (3)*.

MASTERS, ROBERT 'Ditching the Bewitching Myth', in *To Be a Man*, (Keith Thompson)

NOA, JAI 'The Cripple and the Man,' in Baumli, F., (ed) *Men Freeing Men*, New Atlantis Press, 1985.

RINTOUL, STUART 'Initiation', in the *Australian*, Feb 15, 1992.

SIMENON, GEORGES quoted in *Wingspan* (Christopher Harding).

TAYLOR, GEORGE 'Longing for the Great Father', in *Wingspan* (Christopher Harding).

KABIR   quoted in *Iron John* (Robert Bly).

PERKINS, CHARLES quoted by Stuart Rintoul in the *Australian*, Feb 15, 1992.

VENTURA, MICHAEL   'Shadowdancing', quoted in *Wingspan* (Christopher Harding).

Videos

BLY, ROBERT (WITH BILL MOYERS),   'A Gathering of Men', PBS Television.

ALLEN, MARVIN   'Wild Man Weekend', SBS Television.

The People behind the Book

Some of the many people who combined their efforts to produce *Manhood*, Second edition:

1   Steve Biddulph
2&3   Rex and Vicki Finch of Finch Publishing
4   David Hancock, photographer
5   Steve Miller of Snapper Graphics, cover and text design

6&7   David Leslie and Michael Bushell of DOCUPRO, typesetting and page output
8   Robert Stapelfeldt of McPherson's Printing Group
9&10   Howard Taylor and Wendy Livingston of Tower Books, national distribution to bookshops

1

4

2

3

5

6 7

8

9 10

Contacts' List

The following list is accurate at the time of printing, but you know how it is with contact lists.

We have included men's groups (as a good point of initial contact), organisations and a few useful publications.

It is getting easier to link into men's events, groups, conferences and gatherings, as well as just to enquire or get help. Some groups are closed periodically but would be delighted to help you get started with your own.

If you are planning to join a group – trust your instincts, and find one that you feel comfortable with.

The vast majority of men's groups are sensible, down to earth and positive in outlook. Just occasionally you may come across groups that veer into one of two extremes which perhaps should be avoided. There are, on the one hand, some groups calling themselves pro-feminist (but actually meaning 'male apologist') who elevate women into goddesses of purity and light, only to be approached by men crawling on their bellies uttering apologies for existing! And, on the other hand, there are groups comprised of men feeling themselves wounded by women (rightly or wrongly) who simply settle into hating women rather than helping each other heal. And be cautious, too, about New Age profiteering seminars promising to take you into instant warriorhood in a weekend!

The mainstream of the Men's Movement is now wide and strong, and embodies a positive attitude to men and women. The groups listed below are a good place to start.

We hope they will serve as a useful starting point for those wishing to make contact with men's groups or organisations working with men. The list includes groups which are well established. Many other existing groups may not have been listed because they felt their contact addresses were not going to be reliable for the year ahead. Although all contact details were checked before going to press, we are aware that subsequent changes may occur and apologise in advance for any inconvenience caused. Please notify Finch Publishing of any changes: P O Box 120, Lane Cove 2066; phone (02) 9418 6247; fax (02) 9418 8878, email finch@hutch.com.au

Men's groups by region

AUSTRALIAN CAPITAL TERRITORY

Canberra Men's Health and Wellbeing Association (ACT), GPO Box 3172, Canberrra, ACT 2601.

Murringu Canberra Inc., GPO Box 1753, Canberra, ACT 2601. Phone/fax (02) 6239 0666. Support group. Information and referral. Drop-in Tues / Thurs 5.30 - 7 pm at St John's, Reid

NEW SOUTH WALES

Men's Health and Wellbeing Association (NSW) Alun Vaughan, Secretary, PO Box 889, Mona Vale, NSW 2103. Ph 02 9940 1068

Glenbrook Men's Group. Allan Bourke Ph 02 4739 6129

Blue Mountains Men's Network Andrew Chudleigh Ph 02 4758 7672 Offers a central contact point to help with the formation of new groups.

Coffs Harbour Men's Group Bill Hill 8 Crown St, Bellingen, NSW 2454 or Damon Hartman, Ph 02 6651 7129 PO Box 84, Sawtell, NSW 2451.

Gosford / Wyong Central Coast Men's Support Network. Phone/fax Jim Rowe (02) 4329 5005 or 019 454 552.

Hastings district Not Just Us Incorporated. PO Box 1368, Port Macquarie, NSW 2444. Phone Mike Bennett (02) 6584 2532.

Lismore

Open Men's Group Phone Thomas (02) 6624 1069 (ah).

Stuart Anderson (Groups run for men troubled by their violence.) Phone (02) 6622 1441.

Maitland Phone John Towns (02) 4968 2727 or Jeff Sinclair (02) 4932 3178.

Mid Coast Forster Men's Group (Open group), PO Box 69, Forster, NSW 2428. Phone Les McGinniskin (02) 6554 8278.

Murwillumbah Tweed Valley Men's Centre. Phone Ralph Johnston (02) 6679 3194 (hm) or (02) 6672 3003 (ah).

Newcastle Garry Jennings (02) 4956 1453 or Russell Mullins (02) 4956 5883.

Ross Edmonds (02) 4957 5093 or Ross Brown (02) 4957 1671.

Men's Health & Wellbeing Association (Newcastle). Phone Howard James (02) 4982 8928 or Garry Jennings (02) 4956 1453.

Nimbin Michael Katz (02) 6689 1260.

Northern Rivers Mensline, PO Box 1220, Lismore, NSW 2480. Phone (02) 6622 2240.

Nowra region Robert Farnham (02) 4448 7662.

South Coast Moruya Men's Group, 60 Yowani Rd, North Rosedale, NSW 2536. Phone Don Bowak (02) 4471 7124.

Sydney Open Groups, Sydney Men's Network. Several locations. Phone Paul Whyte (02) 9558 9096.

Men's Development Centre, PO Box 815, Rozelle, NSW 2039. Phone Allan Tegg (02) 9569 9296.

Men's Phoneline – Sydney's Community Information and Referral Service for Men. Phone (02) 9979 9909.

The Centre for Men. Phone Norman Dean Radican (02) 9977 7877.

Sydney East Phone Michael Kokot (02) 9365 2974.

Sydney North Mona Vale. Phone Alun Vaughan (02) 9940 1068.

North Sydney Phone Chris (02) 9516 3514.

St Leonards Men's Group. Phone Stuart Stawman (02) 9922 5252.

North Sydney Phone Ben Morphett (02) 9817 7645.

Tweed Heads region Just Men Murwillumbah Incorporated. Phone Marty Rubenstein (07) 5590 9699.

Wyong Wyong Neighbourhood Centre, PO Box 411, Wyong, NSW 2259. Phone Ian Finlayson (02) 4353 1750.

VICTORIA

Men's Health & Wellbeing Association (Vic), PO Box 5053, Alphington, Vic 3078. Phone Phil Morley (03) 9489 1144.

Goulburn Valley Shepparton Men's Group. Stephen Rodgers Ph 03 5828 3426 or Greg Munro Ph 03 5831 2048 (wk) or Robert McLean Ph 03 5822 1766 (hm) 03 5831 2312.

Melbourne Alphington. Phone Robert Ware (03) 9499 5906.

Melbourne Men's Centre. Phone Ash (Andy) Hauser (03) 9417 6142.

Men's Evolvement Network. Phone/fax John Byrne (03) 9499 8969.

Mentor Men's Network. Phone Nick Theophilou (03) 9531 7883.

QUEENSLAND

Men's Health & Wellbeing Association (QLD) 83 Rosalie St, Bardon, QLD 4065. Ph 07 3367 1929

Annerley Tribe of Men. PO Box 324, Stones Corner, QLD 4120. Phone Mal McCouat (07) 3397 1739.

Brisbane Men's Issues Centre. PO Box 272, Carina, Qld 4152. Phone Murray Masarik (07) 3348 8777.

Group For Men. Individual & group therapy. 9 Loch St, West End, Qld 4101 Phone John Lucas (07) 3844 9566.

Cairns Men's Group. Phone Dave Lonergan (070) 517 206.

Capalaba Men's Group. Phone Dave Kohl (07) 3245 4891.

Coolangatta Men's Centre. Open men's groups, helpline. Phone John (07) 5533 8329; or Allan (07) 5533 8257.

Gold Coast North Gold Coast Men's Group. Offers support in a confidential, self-help environment. Phone Leigh (07) 5529 0543.

Mt Tamborine/Beaudesert Contact point for region. Men's 24-hour hotline. Phone Bill Slatter (07) 5545 3519.

Southeast Queensland Men's Helpline. A contact and referral line to men's services. 24 hours, 7 days/week. Brisbane: PO Box 181, Ashgrove, Qld 4060. Brisbane, phone (07) 3830 0055; Gold Coast, phone (07) 5571 8888.

Sunshine Coast SMERI (Suncoast Male Emotions Resource Initiative) Counselling, referrals, male counsellors (7pm - 6am 7 days). PO Box 1099, Maroochydore. Qld 4558. Phone (07) 5443 7534.

SOUTH AUSTRALIA

Adelaide Men's Contact and Resource Centre. PO Box 8036, Adelaide, SA 5001. Phone (08) 8223 1110.

South Australian Men's Movement Inc. (SAMN) Phone Bonnie Gibson (08) 8212 2599.

WESTERN AUSTRALIA

Men's Health & Wellbeing Association (WA) PO Box 744, Claremont, WA 6910. Phone (08) 9279 7381 or Rod Mitchell (08) 9377 1346.

Perth region The MensWork Project, 11 Kirby Way, Samson, WA 6163. Ph/fax Wes Carter (08) 9314 1966.

Men's Confraternity, PO Box 422, Victoria Park, WA 6100. Phone Mike Ward (08) 9470 1734.

TASMANIA

Burnie Northwest Men's Health Action Group. Phone Tony Harris 03 6434 6257.

Hobart region Hobart Men's Group PO Box 431, Sandy Bay, Tas 7005. Phone Simon (03) 6228 6934.

Phone Paul Williams (03) 6233 8728.

Glenorchy Men's Health Unit (and Young Men's Group) Malcolm Tyler, PO Box 572, Glenorchy, Tas 7010. Phone (03) 6233 8723.

Resources

Certified Male A quarterly magazine on men's issues, featuring contributions from men on relationships, fatherhood, the men's movement, sexuality and politics. Locked Bag 1, Springwood, NSW 2777.

Changing Abusive Behaviours Program (Duluth model) Through Centacare Family Services in Hobart, Launceston and Burnie. Contact Tony Bowring: phone (03) 4318 555; fax (03) 4318 114.

Male A bi-annual newsletter/journal on men's issues. PO Box 64, Boronia Park, NSW 2111.

Manhood Online ('Better men for a better world') An Internet on-line magazine, featuring excellent writing and contributions on issues relating to men. Access it at www.manhood.com.au

Men's News A national newsletter for those who work with men, boys and families. PO Box 120, Lane Cove, NSW 2066. Phone (02) 9418 6247; fax (02) 9418 8878. Introductory copy is free.

XY: Men, sex, politics Australian magazine about men and masculinities. P O Box 473, Blackwood SA 5051.

Other Finch Publishing titles

(available through bookshops)

Raising Boys: Why boys are different – and how to help them become happy and well-balanced men (Steve Biddulph). In this bestselling book, Steve Biddulph looks at important issues in boys' development and offers practical suggestions for what we can do to help them enter adulthood as responsible, loving and confident men.

Boys in Schools: Addressing the real issues – behaviour, values and relationships (Editors, Rollo Browne and Richard Fletcher). Positive accounts of how classroom teachers have changed boys' behaviour to improve learning, relationships and the whole-school environment.

Fathers, Sons and Lovers: Men talk about their lives from the 1930s to today (Peter West). Personal stories revealing the changes in men's lives over the past 70 years and an analysis of the issues facing men and boys today.

Men's News A bulletin of men's issues connecting people who work with men and boys in areas such as health, education, counselling and men's groups. Introductory copy is free. Contact Finch Publishing at P O Box 120, Lane Cove 2066 or phone (02) 9418 6247, fax (02) 9418 8878.

Other books by Steve Biddulph

Steve Biddulph has written other significant books on parenting and family relationships: the bestsellers, The *Secret of Happy Children* and *More Secrets of Happy Children* (both published by HarperCollins), *The Making of Love* (published by Doubleday) co-written with Shaaron Biddulph and *The Mother and Baby Book* (published by Murdoch Books) also cowritten with Shaaron Biddulph.

Index

INDEX **259**

Hollows, Fred   164

Industrial Revolution   30, 110
initiation   196–200
   Aboriginal   211–213
   Australian initiation   210
   effects of non-initiation
      200
   false initiation   204
   healing   207
   Kikuyu   197
   meaning of   196, 214
   modern   202
   pain   205
   Perkins, Charles   211–213
   sport   202
   traditional   197, 200, 201
   wounding   203

Jung, C.J.   85, 225

Keen, Sam   87

Lawrence, D.H.   62, 152
Lee, John   107
Leunig, Michael   155, 168–170
Liedloff, Jean   151
loneliness   4, 13
long dark night   96

Mailer, Norman   59
male-out   180
male bashing   34–36
   sexuality   58
   violence   88
marriage fighting in   86
masculinity deep   28
   positive   7
   proving   176
masturbation   63
McKissock, Mal   184
Meade, Michael   127, 206
men accepting help   209
   adolescence   222

approval from fathers   44
childhood wounds   207–209
civilisation   219
communicating feelings
   181
competitiveness   178
comradeship   151
confident maleness   113,
   214
death   7
development   14
elements   214
friendship   186
frustration   101–103
fulfilling work   158–160
grief   184
isolation   4
leaders   164
masturbation   63
media stereotypes   81
modern initiation   197–203
mortgage trap   156
necktie   153
new definitions   182
non-initiation   197
orgasms   58
overcoming obstacles   207
own space   94
persistence and rejection
   92–94
phony   3
power-tactics   244
preventing violence in
   88–91
proving oneself   176
purpose in life   194
raising children   137
relating to women   83
role models   27
separation from boys   29
sexual abuse   68
sexual confidence   68
sexual exploiters   6
sexual identity   70–74